WRITERS AND THEIR WORK

ISOBEL ARMSTRONG
General Editor

BRYAN LOUGHREY
Advisory Editor

Children's Literature

THE MILNE FAMILY
J. V. Milne with his three sons, Barry, Ken and, seated, A. A. Milne.
Following the success of *Little Lord Fauntleroy* in 1886 many children found
themselves similarly dressed in elaborate outfits of velvet and lace.

Children's Literature

in the 1890s and the 1990s

Kimberley Reynolds

Northcote House

in association with
The British Council

First published in 1994 by Northcote House Publishers Ltd, Plymbridge House, Estover Road, Plymouth PL6 7PZ, United Kingdom.
Tel: (0752) 735251. Fax: (0752) 695699.

British Library Cataloguing-in-Publication Data
A catalogue record for this book is available from the British Library

ISBN 0 7463 0728 4

Typeset by Kestrel Data, Exeter
Printed and bound in the United Kingdom by BPC Wheatons Ltd, Exeter

Contents

Illustrations

Acknowledgements

Much of the material for this study has been collected for courses I teach at Roehampton Institute with the help of a number of colleagues. I would like particularly to thank Pat Pinsent, who read the manuscript and who has been a marvellous colleague over the years. In the library, Felicity Lander has been especially helpful, locating material and helping to develop the Children's Literature Centre. Bryan Loughrey has created a number of opportunities for me to put my ideas in print; I am particularly glad that he finally found a publisher who is interested in children's literature! Nicholas Tucker has, throughout my career, been a supportive friend and colleague. Thanks are also due to my good friend, Paul Yates, whose advice and support are very important to me. As always, my husband, Peter Reynolds, advised me on the project, read the manuscript, and helped make it possible for me to find the time to write it.

The author and publishers are grateful for permission to reproduce the following copyright material:

Pages 12-13 from *MAUS I: A Survivor's Tale* by Art Spiegelman (Penguin Books, 1987) Copyright © Art Spiegelman, 1973, 1980, 1981, 1982, 1983, 1984, 1985, 1986. Reproduced by permission of the author and Penguin Books Ltd.; *Marianne Dreams* by permission of Catherine Storr and Faber and Faber Ltd.; Kate Greenaway's 'Wishes' from the *The Golden Age of Children's Book Illustration* by Richard Dalby, published by Michael O'Mara Books; *Wolf* by Gillian Cross (OUP, 1990) by permission of the author and Oxford University Press; *Watching Roses* by Adele Geras by permission of the author and HarperCollins Publishers Limited; *Piggybook* © Anthony Browne, published in the UK by Walker Books Limited; *Bill's New Frock* by Anne Fine and *The*

Lives of Christopher Chant by Diana Wynne Jones by permission of the authors and the publishers, Mammoth; *Spring-Heeled Jack* by permission of Philip Pullman and the publishers, Yearling Books, Transworld Publishers Ltd.; extract and illustrations from *The Stinky Cheese Man & Other Fairly Stupid Tales* by John Scieszka and Lane Smith. Copyright © John Scieszka and Lane Smith 1992. Reproduced by permission of Penguin Books Ltd. Extracts from the novels *Breaktime* and *The Toll Bridge*, both by Aidan Chambers, are quoted by permission of the author and the publisher, The Bodley Head (Random House UK Ltd.). Marjorie Murray-Rust, niece of A. A. Milne, for the frontispiece photograph of her father and his family in his youth.

Introduction

Children's literature is often dismissed as literature written by those who can't write any better for those who can't read any better. The following study is intended to disprove both of these assumptions by looking at the quality and diversity of writing for young people over the past 100 years. As well as showing that a great deal of children's literature is *good* literature which can withstand any kind of critical scrutiny, I have attempted to show that whatever its literary merit, children's literature is an important phenomenon for several reasons. First, reading is inextricably bound up with language and language acquisition, and it is through language that we understand and construct the world. While reading, the young person is trying out new languages, experimenting with different kinds of subject positions and iden- tities, and encountering different ideas about what the world feels like.

Another reason why children's literature is important is that in our society reading is an activity which is valued by the majority of the population, and certainly by major institutions. The most obvious forum in which reading comes to the fore is school, and it is not accidental that by far and away the majority of books for young readers are highly instructive. This means that what is being read is deeply implicated in the kinds of values and ideas the child learns to hold about society. No literature is neutral, but children's literature is more concerned with shaping its readers' attitudes than most. Therefore, if we are interested in under- standing how our society works – where young people get their attitudes about issues such as sex, gender, violence, government, and war – it behoves us to look at what is being read.

The dialectical interaction between social policy and children's literature is a fascinating and fruitful area of study, which I have only briefly touched on here, as the nature of this exercise has been to provide an overview of the issues and narrative techniques of children's literature. Indeed, in a study of this kind it is impossible to provide a panoramic view of children's literature. Accordingly, I have had to be selective, trying to focus on what is either representative, influential, or ground-breaking. This policy has resulted in some conspicuous absences – there is very little here about historical fiction or fantasy for instance. The reason for this is that these are areas which have been thoroughly discussed elsewhere (sources are provided in the suggestions for further reading).

The reason for looking at literature of the *fin de siècle* periods was that it made it possible to show that many of the underlying premises about writing for children at the end of the twentieth century have their roots in social practice and publishing decisions in operation at the end of the nineteenth century. The tenacity of these anachronistic influences is explored here, as well as attempts to bring children's literature into the twentieth century – succeeding more or less as we leave it! Throughout this study I try to make *fin de siècle* mean the final decade of the century, but, as all historians know, it is impossible to stick rigidly within any pair of dates and accurately trace the growth of an idea or attitude. There are a number of instances when I have wanted to include material which has either been influential in one of the *fin de siècle* periods, or seems to represent its concerns despite the fact that it was written before that period. *Fin de siècle* here is as much a state of mind or quality of writing as a historical moment.

Many people write about children's literature, and even the child who might be reading it, without thinking about the relationship between real childhood, real children, and their literary representation. In recent years attention has been focused on the relationship between the adult writer and the child reader. While this has been fruitful, and certainly informs any study of literary childhood, it is also important to think about the real children who read books and the kinds of lives they are likely to lead. For this reason, I have tried always to relate the texts being discussed to theories of childhood and historical evidence about childhood.

Finally, 'children's literature' as a label has always been problematic; not least because its intended audience is so large and varied. The problem has been increased in the closing decades of this century by publishers' efforts to extend the genre by adding on new – and often very exciting – titles for teenage readers. Specialist bookshops, publishers' catalogues, many libraries, and courses on children's literature use the label to mean anything which is not marketed as adult fiction. This means that picture books and complex novels jockey for position in the same spaces. As this is standard practice, despite its paradoxes and short-comings, this is what I have done here. One result is that picture books have been given relatively little attention in this study. This reflects pragmatic thinking (to discuss picture books adequately you need to use many illustrations), but also the fact that recently several good studies of picture books have been published. These are discussed in the suggestions for further reading in the bibliography. The same applies to poetry, games, and the words and rituals associated with the folklore of childhood.

Despite these notable absences, the following pages provide a general overview of the history and development of children's literature in Great Britain. I should add that a few of the books discussed were written by American authors and first published in the United States. Because they are also published in the UK and are well established as part of the mainstream of juvenile fiction in Britain, it seems important to acknowledge their influence on young people's reading in this country as well.

While the emphasis of this study is on literature for young readers, I try also to show that childhood and children's literature are in a dialectical relationship: as childhood is prolonged through improvements in living conditions, medicine, and affluence, it takes on a new meaning for adult writers. When childhood was relatively brief and maturity full of uncertainty, many adults seem to have wanted to relive and renegotiate their own childhoods. As the boundaries between adult and child become more and more blurred, however, a number of writers have begun to use children's literature as a way of facilitating the maturing process and fostering independence. As Stephen Spielberg's *Hook* proves, ambivalence about the relationship between adult and childish selves as well as between adult and child continues to dominate our thinking about children and children's literature.

1

Forever Young: Fantasies of Childhood

All children, except one, grow up. They soon know that they will grow up, and the way Wendy knew was this. One day when she was two years old she was playing in a garden, and she plucked another flower and ran with it to her mother. I suppose she must have looked rather delightful, for Mrs Darling put her hand to her heart and cried, 'Oh why can't you remain like this for ever!' This was all that passed between them on the subject, but henceforth Wendy knew that she must grow up. You always know after you are two. Two is the beginning of the end. (*Peter Pan*, p. 13)

CHILDHOOD AND CHILDREN'S LITERATURE

The end of the nineteenth century, the period widely known as the *fin de siècle*, is often painted as a brief, riotous reaction to the repressive social regimes of Victorian Britain, and a decadent falling away from its high moral tone and preoccupation with classical culture. The outrageously extrovert behaviour of Oscar Wilde, the beautiful perversion of Aubrey Beardsley's drawings and erotica, the determination of a public élite to saturate the senses and so escape the *ennui* of everyday life characterize the popular image of this period. The quintessential *fin de siècle* character is, of course, Oscar Wilde's Dorian Gray. Gray is the original Peter Pan – the boy who won't grow up – and in him it is possible to locate one of the central facets of the *fin de siècle Weltanschauung*: the adult's ambivalent feelings about childhood. At the end of the last century, childhood was regarded as both naïvely beautiful and brutishly threatening. From where did this

1

ambivalence originate? To understand the *fin de siècle* schizophrenia towards children it's necessary to look back to the middle of the century, to the time when those who were parents in the 1890s were themselves children.

It is not true (though often said) that the Victorians invented childhood as we know it, or even that theirs was the first period simultaneously to idolize and resent its children. These antagonistic feelings no doubt go back as far as human society.[1] However, in the course of Queen Victoria's long and full reign (1837-1901) the middle and upper classes evolved a more self-conscious and sustained myth of childhood than any that had gone before. This myth was in large measure the product of social practice, which meant that most parents from these classes had very little to do with the day-to-day care of their offspring. Servants were largely responsible for bathing, dressing, entertaining, and disciplining the children of the house, formally presenting them to their parents, scrubbed and instructed to be on their best behaviour, at agreed times (a practice which was to continue at least until the First World War). There were many potential consequences of this pattern of child-rearing. For instance, Leonore Davidoff[2] has suggested that because children's affective relationships were often with servants rather than parents, as adults they found it difficult to relate physically to members of their own class. Parent-child relationships were characterized by formality, and fathers in particular associated with authoritarian behaviour. The problem seems to have been particularly acute for upper- and middle-class boys, who were generally sent away from home to attend preparatory schools by age 7 or 8, prior to taking up places at public boarding schools at 13. Boys were brought up to respect their fathers and to revere their mothers – the 'angels of the house'.

The problems and tensions engendered for many children by living under the shadow of these remote and immaculate paragons is encapsulated by Frederick Robertson, who grew up under this kind of regime:

> The beings that floated before me, robed in vestures more delicate than mine, were beings of another order. The thought of one of them becoming mine was not rapture but pain . . . At seven years old,

woman was a sacred dream, of which I would not talk. Marriage was a degradation.[3]

Because women of their own class (certainly the women you married) were understood to be untouchable, and conditioned to think of themselves as lacking in sexual passion (the psychology and politics of women's passionlessness are discussed more fully in Nancy F. Cott, 'Passionlessness', and Reynolds and Humble, *Victorian Heroines*),[4] it seems that many Victorian and Edwardian men felt more comfortable with working-class women, girl children, or with other men. Accordingly, one manifestation of this phenomenon was the widespread use of prostitutes and the frequent seduction of servants; another, grown men's passions for young girls (perhaps most famously John Ruskin's for Rose La Touche), and a third the dependence on and institutionalization of all-male environments such as the boys' public school, the military, the civil service, and the private club.[5] A final and more general symptom of the problem which is particularly evident in the literature of *fin de siècle* Britain was the sense that relationships between the sexes were in crisis. Each of these is a large, complex issue, the intricacies of which go beyond the bounds of this discussion (suggestions for further reading are provided in the bibliography). They do, however, form a necessary background on which to trace the outline of the *fin de siècle* myth of childhoood, for if Victorian children were encouraged to regard their parents as omnipotent and ideal, bourgeois households elevated childhood to unprecedented heights. Just as the pattern of distance-parenting was capable of concealing parents' foibles and failings, so it tended to present only the pretty and angelic face of childhood to parents, leaving the tantrums and tedium to their full-time carers. Moreover, the influential discourses of Romanticism, which emphasized the child's natural innocence and creativity, intensified parents' infatuation with the idea of their children and the period of childhood.

This celebratory attitude to childhood came to prominence in the middle years of the century; the very moment when *fin de siècle* parents were entering the world. For the remainder of the century the myth of childhood became increasingly elaborate; particularly in representations of children in literature and art. An enduring consequence of it has been an exaggerated and unrealistic sense of difference between adult and child, which most of us experience as a sense of crisis and discontinuity in adolescence, when the difference needs to be traversed.[6] This often results in the feeling that growing up involves the loss of special qualities that may never be recovered. It also sets up peculiar and unrealistic paradoxes between the states and status of adult and child. Ruth Benedict puts it thus:

> our culture goes to great extremes in emphasizing contrasts between the child and the adult. The child is sexless, the adult estimates his virility by his sexual activities; the child must be protected from the ugly facts of life, the adult must meet them without psychic catastrophe; the child must obey, the adult must command this obedience. (*Psychiatry*, 1, 1938, p. 161)

For Benedict, the importance of this discontinuity is the fact that it is culturally constructed. There are, of course, physiological and developmental differences between adults and children, but at different historical moments and in different cultures the emphasis has been (and is) on the *continuity* between childhood and maturity. For instance, when books were first being printed in Britain (Caxton set up his press in 1476), it was widely believed that the embryo was essentially a miniature adult, or homunculus, and that childhood was primarily the period during which the small adult became large. This was one reason why very few books were written for children. There *were* simple books which we may now regard as early examples of 'children's literature' – Caxton's *Aesop's Fables* for instance – but their simplicity was intended to help inexperienced readers of all ages rather than specifically the child reader. When the skills and interests of adults and children converge in this manner, the child is understood to be preparing to become an adult, and consequently to have within him or herself most of the feelings and drives which come to fruition in maturity. The idea that childhood is characterized by its difference from maturity in being a uniquely 'innocent' phase which must be preserved, prolonged, and protected, is very much a product of the Victorian period (though subsequently the ideas of Freud have contributed further to modern-day preoccupations with the importance of childhood). It stems in part from the parenting practices described above, but a range of other factors were also instrumental.

One key area which needs to be considered is the relationship between childhood and capitalism. At its most basic level, childhood became more important under industrial capitalism as an increasing number of parents had money and property to pass on to their children. While lacking any direct access to capital themselves, children were both the inheritors of and reasons for accumulating and *spending* wealth. This resulted in two equally important components in the evolving image of childhood. First, as Roland Barthes points out in his essay 'Toys',[7] the objects we produce and purchase for children function largely to instruct the children of the bourgeoisie in the values and ideologies which maintain them. Thus, as Barthes observes, little girls are traditionally given toys which help to feminize and condition them for house-keeping and motherhood, and boys those which prepare them for such things as war and bureaucracy. This was true in the 1890s, and remains true in the 1990s, despite ever growing concern that a child's biological sex should not be used as the dominant factor which determines the experiences and opportunities available to boys and girls as they grow up. This is a good example of what the French Marxist philosopher, Louis Althusser, calls an Ideological State Apparatus (ISA) in operation.

Althusser has provided a detailed explanation of how ideology works, showing that ideology (how we perceive and understand the world around us) is not just – or even primarily – comprised of consciously held political opinions, but pervades all the institutions and structures of society: schools, churches, the family, legal and political systems, and so on. It is also built into the language we speak so that in order to participate in society we always and inevitably start by understanding ourselves as subjects within it. Because we internalize its views and value systems it is hard not to see them as natural, and even harder to change them. Understanding the nature of ideology is important when considering the role and development of children's literature at any time for, as Stephens argues, children's literature is particularly revealing in what he calls its 'struggle for young people's minds'.[8] The attitudes and positions proffered in the literature produced for young readers tell us a great deal about the preoccupations and values of the time. It is particularly important to be aware of the pressures at work at the end of the last century, for it is then that the foundations of the juvenile publishing industry as we know it were laid.[9] Many of the decisions made then (for instance, to create separate literary genres for boys and girls) persist into the 1990s even though they reflect particular social conditions which are no longer appropriate at the end of the twentieth century. Their staying power is a reflection of their grounding in the economics of industrial capitalism.

Accordingly, another important aspect of the rise in the social status of childhood (also related to the needs of capitalist society) was the recognition that parents enjoyed indulging their children (and their own fantasies of what children were like) through purchasing books, toys, novelties, and clothes. An industry developed to service this taste, which reached a crescendo as far as children's clothing was concerned just before the *fin de siècle* proper, with the publication of Frances Hodgson Burnett's *Little Lord Fauntleroy* (1885-6). Parents across Great Britain and the United States dressed their children in Fauntleroy-inspired costumes of velvet with elaborate lace collars, and boys and girls alike were forced to have their hair curled in ringlets in imitation of the novel's 7-year-old hero, Cedric Errol, whose own 'bright curly hair . . . waved over his forehead and fell in charming love-locks on his shoulders' (ch. 1, p. 10).

Little Lord Fauntleroy shows clearly the relationship between children's literature and the social status and image of childhood. Before the cult of the beautiful child,[10] however, a very different understanding of childhood dominated British society and books for children. Perhaps the most influential and best-known example of this earlier image is provided by Mrs Mary Martha Sherwood's (1775-1851) ubiquitous history of *The Fairchild Family* (1818). Sherwood's text is firmly rooted in both the didactic and Calvinistic traditions. She wrote not to entertain youngsters, but to instruct them, and instruction she felt they needed, for Mrs Sherwood belonged to the influential body of opinion (largely derived from Puritanism) which held that every child comes into the world branded with the mark of Original Sin. It was, therefore, every adult's duty (and particularly every parent's) to ensure that children recognized the error of their sinful ways, repented, and turned to God. It was felt never to be too early to begin this process, for child mortality was extremely high and parents were desperate to ensure that their babies were in a state of grace before they were called. Thus parents felt it right and necessary to

Shock-headed Peter

Just look at him! there he stands,
With his nasty hair and hands.
See! his nails are never cut;
They are grimed as black as soot;
And the sloven, I declare,
Never once has combed his hair;
Anything to me is sweeter
Than to see Shock-headed Peter.

Dr Heinrich Hoffman's famous 'Shock-headed Peter'.

chastise their children – even young babies – in ways which seem excessive and often gratuitous by present-day standards. (The extent to which this emphasis on punishment can be understood to be a sadistic product of the parents' own upbringing is discussed in G. Rattray Taylor, *The Angel Makers* and C. J. Sommerville, *The Discovery of Childhood in Puritan England*.[11])

A vivid example of the Calvinistic determination not to 'spare the rod and spoil the child', as well as the concerns which preoccupy loving parents throughout the ages, is provided in the *Journals* (1886) of Thomas Cobden-Sanderson, who describes the methods he employed for controlling his 18-month-old son:

> Our anxiety for his future makes us careful in ridding him of bad habits and making his will 'supple' as Locke – whom we are now reading – would say. The other night he cried after being put to bed, not of course from pain, but mere contrariness. I tried to induce him to be quiet and failed. I then took him out of bed and whipped him, and as he cried out even more, pressed him close to me, and held his head and bade him to be quiet. In a moment, after a convulsive sob or two, he became quite quiet. I put him back into his cot, told him to be quiet and to go to sleep, and left him. Not a sound more did he make, and he went to sleep. The next day at noon he cried again when put to bed. I went to him and told him he must not cry, that he must lie down[. . .]be quiet and go to sleep.[. . .]He became and remained perfectly quiet, and went to sleep. He now goes to bed noon and night and to sleep without a cry. If this can be done, how much more may not be done? What a responsibility! What a superb instrument, gymnast of virtue and of beautiful conduct, may not a man be made early in life.[12]

Mrs Sherwood's concerns are very similar; in *The Fairchild Family* (widely read throughout the last century) she set out to show the rewards of parental success and the consequences for children whose parents fail to make them 'gymnasts of virtue'. It centres around the activities of the Fairchilds – a model family headed by a husband and wife who live in accordance with all the precepts of Calvinism. They live moderately in a pastoral world 'very far from any town'; are neither high nor low, carry out their duties, at home and in the community, responsibly, and set about teaching their children (and thus those who read the book) 'the importance and effects of a religious education'.

The Fairchild Family is renowned for its many and various

accounts of childhood death. A typical contrast of successful versus unsuccessful parenting is provided by the deaths of Miss Augusta Noble (spoiled daughter of the local gentry), and that of the Fairchild's servants' son, little Charles Trueman. In one of the most famous episodes in the book (story number 16, 'Fatal Effects of Disobedience to Parents'), Mrs Fairchild and her children are told of Augusta's death by their neighbour, Mrs Barker:

'Ah, Mrs. Fairchild, the manner of her death is the worst part of the story, and that which must grieve her parents' hearts. You know that poor Miss Augusta was always the darling of her mother, who brought her up in great pride, without fear of God or knowledge of religion; nay, Lady Noble would even mock at religion and religious people in her presence; and she chose a governess for her who had no more of God about her than herself.[. . .]As Miss Augusta was brought up without the fear of God,' continued Mrs. Barker, 'she had, of course, no notion of obedience to her parents, farther than just striving to please them in their presence; she lived in the constant practice of disobeying them.[. . .]'

The Noble parents had forbidden their daughter to play with candles and matches, but, because of her upbringing, Augusta ignored their instructions. The consequences were that one night, when her parents were playing cards (a sure sign of their own fallen state), she took a candle and began to look at herself in the mirror (vanity being another of her sins). The maid, Mrs Barker continued,

'was frightened by dreadful screamings[. . .]and[. . .]found poor Augusta all in a blaze, from head to foot.[. . .]and.[. . .]so dreadfully burnt, that she never spoke afterwards, but died in agonies last night – a warning to all children how they presume to disobey their parents! 'The eye that mocketh at his father, and refuses to obey his mother, the ravens of the valley shall pick it out, and the young eagles shall eat it.' (Prov. xxx, 17)

When reading a text from the past, and particularly one which is specifically concerned with child-rearing (and so is explicitly interested in integrating young people into society), it is often easier to recognize its ideological biases than it is with texts from our own period, but it is important to remember that *all* texts are ideological – the products of particular historical circumstances and opinions. If we fail to notice the ideological stance of a contemporary text, it is because its messages are in accordance with our own point of view and therefore seem natural. Strange though it may seem to us now, the attitudes and lessons which characterize Mrs Sherwood's text also seemed natural and like common sense to most of her readers. The change in our response to *The Fairchild Family* usefully illustrates the point that ideology is not just something that is done to us, but it is also part of us. Thus, when reading any text, there is always an interaction between the sociocultural values of the author and those of the reader: those inscribed in the text and those which the reader brings to it.[13]

But compatible ideologies in themselves do not produce enduring bestsellers. A more important reason for Mrs Sherwood's success can be found in her story-telling techniques. Looking through the brief extract above we may be struck by its undisguised religiosity and overtly didactic tone and may assume that children would have found it tedious. Compared to the majority of the literature available to them, however (for remember, in 1818 there was very little in the way of children's literature), *The Fairchild Family* was full of exciting occurrences (children being burned to death, dead men hanging on gibbets, an assortment of punishments – which the young reader would have been glad to have escaped – and so on) and an interesting range of narrative techniques. As the extract shows, Mrs Sherwood enjoyed incorporating dialogue in her stories, and also other kinds of voices. The quotation from Proverbs is characteristic, and to the child who had to memorize a hymn, collect and/or prayer each Sunday, her allusions to each of these biblical or religious forms of writing would often have been familiar and empowering rather than tedious. Sherwood is writing intertextually – a narrative technique which has always featured prominently in children's literature (and to which I will return later).

The range of Sherwood's allusions also helps to underpin the text's ideology. Throughout *The Fairchild Family* the author assumes the reader shares her values and opinions, and this is conveyed by the text's modality (its attitudes and level of conviction, most easily seen in words or phrases such as 'of course', 'naturally' and 'undoubtedly', which encourage us to accept the narrator's point of view). There are no uncertainties in Sherwood's writing – no hesitations, gaps, or weaknesses which stand out and allow the reader, even momentarily to step back from its world view. For instance, even her use of intertextuality does not disrupt the text but draws on authoritative works to enforce its messages. That we can now be more objective is almost entirely because there has been a cultural shift in our attitude to childhood which makes the central tenets of *The Fairchild Family* both unfamiliar and repugnant to many modern readers (though in 1993 there are vociferous organizations which are pressing for a return to many of the values expressed by Mrs Sherwood – not least the idea that both parents and the state have a right and a duty physically to punish children in order to make them better citizens). This shift in our attitude and understanding of childhood directly affects the way we read this and other similar texts, for the attitudes which once seemed natural and so effaced themselves as part of the reading process now seem crude and manipulative.

Before leaving *The Fairchild Family*, it is important to look at one other aspect of its teachings – its attitude to childhood death – as in this area, too, a huge shift in attitude occurred during the second half of the century. Sherwood ends her text with the death of little Charles Trueman. He lies on his deathbed surrounded by family and friends, anticipating heaven, and though the scene is moving, it is not sad. The reason for this is that Sherwood belonged to the school which taught that the death of a child who had achieved a state of grace (unlike Augusta Noble) was not to be mourned but should be regarded as the happiest moment in that child's life. The logic behind this was that having been on earth just long enough to repent and turn to God, but not long enough to build up a catalogue of sins, the child would return all the more readily and fully to his or her father in heaven. According to this model, Charles's death is exemplary:

> A few days before Christmas the weather became very cold, and a great change at the same time took place in little Charles. Mr. and Mrs. Fairchild[. . .]notwithstanding the hard frost, often went to see him as he drew nearer to his end, and were much pleased with the happy state of mind in which he was, for he seemed to have no desire but to be with Him who had died for him, even that Lamb of God which was slain for the sins of the world. Early one Wednesday morning, in the beginning of the month of December, a neighbour came over in haste to Mr. Fairchild's to call Henry: 'Little Charley is

11

dying,' she said, 'and asks for young Master.' As soon as Mr. Fairchild and the family heard the news, they all set off in haste.[. . .]Poor little Charles was lying on a bed in his grandmother's room. His head was lying on a pillow, supported by his mother, who sat upon the bed looking at her dying child, whilst her tears ran down her cheeks. John Trueman was kneeling on one side of the bed, holding one of Charles's hands . . . and poor Charles's elder brother and sister were crying in different parts of the room.

When Mr. and Mrs. Fairchild came in, Charles's eyes were shut, and he lay as if sleeping. He was much changed since the day before: his eyes were sunk, his face become deadly pale, and his mouth drawn close. When Henry looked at him, he could keep his tears back no longer. . . . After a few minutes Charles opened his eyes, and looked round him at every one.[. . .]

'Do not cry Master Henry,' said Charles, speaking in a low voice; 'I am happy.'

'And what makes you happy now, dear boy?' said Mr. Somers [the clergyman]; 'speak and tell us, that we may all here present lay fast hold of the same Hope, which is able to make a dying bed so easy.'

Charles turned his dying eyes towards Mr. Somers, and answered: 'I know that my Redeemer liveth; and though after my skin worms shall destroy this body, yet in my flesh I shall see God.' (Job, xix, 25, 26)

The semiotics of this scene need hardly to be unpacked. The young boy's death deliberately evokes the death of Christ. Indeed, his deathbed, significantly set in the Christmas period, appropriately contains elements of both Christ's birth (to low-born parents who honour Him) and His death, as Sherwood's description of the mother cradling her dying son creates a kind of *pietà*. Equally important is the fact that Charles's death is reassuring, not distressing. The text stresses that because he has lived a blameless life and sought God's grace his passage to heaven is simple. Already he is hovering between this world and the next, and his final words, which promise eternal life in God's presence, confirm the teachings of the Fairchild parents. Young Henry is particularly moved by the death of his working-class counterpart, and this is appropriate for a future defender of the empire who must believe that 'death rather than dishonour' is always the best course.

The emphasis on instruction characteristic of *The Fairchild Family* continued throughout Victoria's reign (and many would argue that it has never disappeared from writing for children[14]); how-ever, the purpose and nature of the lessons included in writing for children changed radically. Foucault identified the capacity for systems of belief, including those by which a culture con-ceptualizes itself, to be radically revised over a short period of time: 'within the space of a few years a culture sometimes ceases to think as it had been thinking up till then and begins to think in a new way'.[15] Superficially, at least, this seems to have been true of the Victorian attitude to childhood, for by the middle years of the century the Calvinistic preoccupation with Original Sin was replaced by a new image of childhood and a complete reversal in the roles and responsibilities inherent in parent-child relation-ships. Whereas previously the child was thought to be innately wicked and requiring parental guidance and chastisement for his/her salvation, now, largely through the popularization of the theories of Jean Jacques Rousseau (1712–78), Victorian society began to think of the child not as wicked, but as the pure, blameless link to the prelapsarian world. (Rousseau's famous treatise on the education and upbringing of children, *Emile*, was first published in 1760, and though it was immediately translated into English and influenced many writers for children, the impact of his theories was not widely disseminated for nearly a century.) In this new version of childhood, what the child acquired through instruction and experience of the world was not a state of grace, but a loss of perfection – the consequence of contact with what Rousseau pejoratively termed 'civilization'.

This new image of childhood both empowered and sentimen-talized the child – or at least the child in fiction and art – whose clarity of vision was understood to be capable of exposing adult hypocrisy and wrong doing. Accordingly, the children at the centre of juvenile fiction were no longer impotent and insigni-ficant. Rather, each was invested with the capacity to set the world to rights and lead fallen adults back to the paths of righteousness and salvation. This image of childhood finds its apotheosis in the work of evangelical writers such as Hesba Stretton (1832–1911), a founder member of the London Society for the Prevention of Cruelty to Children. For instance, in her bestselling story *Little Meg's Children* (1868), the central character single-handedly nurses and buries her mother; then, while living in the worst kind of London slum, cares for her young siblings, redeems a prostitute

13

and reunites her with her grieving mother, reforms a drunkard father, and manages to bring all those with whom she comes in touch closer to God – despite the fact that she has had no formal religious education herself and, like many of Stretton's characters, is even uncertain about how to pray. Indeed, one of Stretton's most successful books was called *Jessica's First Prayer* (1867), and the following extract captures well both Stretton's glorification of the child and her concern with the living conditions of children in London's slums. In this scene, which comes near the end of the book, Jessica has been abandoned by her alcoholic mother, who fears she has a contagious disease, and left their 'home'. Here she is found by Daniel, a miser who is torn between his desire to earn money and his desire for social status, which requires that he appear not to work:

> The child was lying in desolate darkness.[. . .]She was stretched upon a scanty litter of straw under the slanting roof where the tiles had not fallen off, with her poor rags for her only covering. . . .
> 'Oh!' she cried gladly, but in a feeble voice, 'It's Mr. Dan'el! Has God told you to come here, Mr. Dan'el?'
> 'Yes,' said Daniel, kneeling beside her, taking her wasted hand in his, and parting the matted hair upon her damp forehead.[. . .]'He told me I was a great sinner.[. . .]He told me I loved a little bit of dirty money better than a poor friendless, helpless child, whom he had sent to see if I would do her a little good for His sake.[. . .]'
> 'Why don't you ask him to make you good for Jesus Christ's sake?' asked the child.
> 'I can't,' he said.[. . .]
> By the feeble glimmer of the candle Daniel saw Jessica's wistful eyes fixed upon him with a sad and loving glance; and then she lifted up her weak hand to her face, and laid it over her closed eyelids, and her feverish lips moved slowly.
> 'God,' she said, 'please to make Mr. Daniel's heart soft, for Jesus Christ's sake. Amen.'

And of course he does. Daniel takes Jessica home with him where she recovers and they live together happily ever after (the ne'er-do-well mother having disappeared permanently).

The sentimentality of Stretton's portrayal of childhood is typical of the age and, while it is firmly rooted in realistic circumstances (Stretton visited the slums and worked energetically to help the poor women and children she found trapped there), it also helps elaborate the Victorian mythology of incorruptible childhood. It is important to note that while the simplicity of the language used and the fact that a child is at the centre of each of Stretton's best-known stories made them well suited for children, they were not specifically or exclusively for children. Indeed, Stretton's work was widely read and she received many letters from adults of all kinds and in every circumstance who were moved by the plight of her young characters. Her emphasis on childhood as a time of moral safety and security and the reliable way in which her plots reward the just and forgive the erring seemed to strike a deep chord in the second half of the last century. Perhaps this was because Stretton, and writers like her, combined real issues with fictional children and so seemed to suggest the possibility of solutions to what appeared to be insoluble problems. Whatever the reason, their romantic treatment of fictional childhood was to complement similar portrayals by well-respected writers such as Charles Dickens, and help underpin the changing image of childhood in late-Victorian society.

The significance of this shift in the social meaning of childhood is twofold. First, it makes childhood immensely powerful and good, and so the proper subject for nostalgia (no right-thinking adult would previously have thought it right to admit to a desire to return to a time associated with sinfulness, and since childhood had previously been experienced largely as a stage to be got through as quickly and with as few punishments as possible, it is unlikely to have been a time most would have wanted to revisit in any case). The second important aspect of this shift is that the elevation of childhood, and the fact that it was increasingly being linked to a notional Golden Age, brought with it new pleasures and security. At no time before had there been anything to rival the comforts and diversity provided by the Victorian nursery. Thus, it seems likely that those children raised in the middle years of the century and who were themselves *fin de siècle* parents were more susceptible to exaggerated feelings about the importance of childhood than any generation before them. This would in itself account for the pre-eminence of fantasies and myths of childhood, but additional factors strengthened this tendency.

Perhaps the most immediately influential cause of the intensification and increased sentimentality of the image of childhood was the appalling rate of infant and child mortality at the end of the century. Indeed, this period saw the worst infant mortality rate ever recorded: 163 out of every 1,000 births, and of those who survived their first year, a quarter died before they reached the age of 5.[16] Horrific though these figures are, however, child death had always been known, and influential historians such as Philippe Ariès have argued that in fact high rates of childhood death result in quite a different response. In *Centuries of Childhood*, Ariès argues that when the arrival of a child was often an annual event in families, and parents expected to lose at least half of their children, it was emotionally impossible to feel as attached to each as parents do today. Whether or not Ariès is right, the increasing infant mortality rate does not provide an adequate explanation for the new cult of childhood. One very important reason for this is that the elevation of childhood was primarily a middle-class phenomenon, but in the middle classes childhood deaths were actually decreasing. Consequently, it is necessary to look beyond simple causality for a more complex social explanation of the phenomenon; it is probable that the new cult of childhood owed more to a general sense of dislocation and unease.

The *fin de siècle* was characterized by its self-consciousness, including its consciousness of living through an age of profound change and transition. The future no longer seemed knowable and predictable, and many of the assumptions which had under-pinned British culture (for instance, Christianity, patriarchy, and British imperialism) were being radically challenged. The middle-class retreat into the family (an option largely denied to the working class at this time) can be understood as symptomatic of the phenomenon the contemporary practitioner of the new discipline of anthropology, Emile Durkheim (1858–1917), labelled *anomie*. Durkheim originally used the term to refer to a syndrome he identified in the urban working class, but with the advantage of hindsight it can be seen to have wider implications, for essentially *anomie* means a lack of certainty about the social organization and norms of society and the way oneself and/or one's group fits into them. Previously social rules, expectations, and beliefs were, if anything, *too* well known and prescriptive. Now they seemed to be changing and challenged in every sphere – by women, by scientists, by theologians, by the Aesthetes, and, as far as children were concerned, by the government, which, among other things, legislated them out of work, off the streets, and into schools.[17] Given the sense of constant change and the fear that it was leading towards social disintegration and disaster, it is no wonder that so many *fin de siècle* writers and artists explored what it would be like to be able to control time or turn the clock back.

CHILDHOOD AS ADULT FANTASY

That the *fin de siècle* nostalgia for childhood must be understood to be an *adult* preoccupation (most children at any time are only too anxious to grow up) is evident in that it is in books originally written for adult audiences that the fantasy of defying or controlling time (or the effects of maturity) first manifests itself. In addition to Wilde's *The Picture of Dorian Gray*, typical examples of this phenomenon are H. G. Wells's *The Time Machine* (1895), Henry James's *What Maisie Knew* (1897), and, just as the century turned, J. M. Barrie's *The Little White Bird* (1902), which contains the original story of Peter Pan (F. Anstey's *Vice-Versa, or, a Lesson to Fathers* (1882) is an interesting pre-*fin de siècle* example more specifically intended to appeal to children as well as adults). This trend is so pronounced and so central to the literature of this period that it could be said that the subsequent modernist preoccupations with time and memory are essentially elaborations (fuelled by the theories of Freud, Bergson, and Einstein) of the *fin de siècle* impulse to resist the social and biological imperatives to grow up and cope with the new world.

It is important to remember that ambivalence about growing up was an attitude which affected only a minority of the population, though this minority was responsible for providing most of the stories and images of late-Victorian and Edwardian childhood which have become our 'children's classics'. For most of the population, childhood continued to be an inconvenient, often brutal, phase to be got through as quickly as possible. From the 1890s to the First World War, working-class childhood officially ended on a young person's twelfth birthday – the legal working age (though at least part-time attendance at school was required until 14). Unofficially it often ended much earlier; especially in large families. As Hesba Stretton showed in *Little Meg's Children*, girls as young as 7 or 8 were often left in charge of younger

17

brothers and sisters while their parents went out to work, and even the youngest members of the family were expected to contribute to its income by helping with piece work, running errands, or in any other way possible. Despite changes in educational policy which since 1880 had required children to attend school, attendance was likely to be erratic – subject to the vagaries of mothers' confinements, opportunities for paid employment, weather (particularly in rural areas where children would often have inadequate clothing for long journeys), and for those living in the country, the seasonal demands for their labour on the land. For working-class children living in the cities, life at the end of the century had often changed little from that Henry Mayhew observed fifty years earlier and documented in his account of the Watercress Girl[18].

> The little watercress girl who gave me the following statement, although only eight years of age, had entirely lost all childish ways, and was, indeed, in thoughts and manner, a woman. There was something cruelly pathetic in hearing this infant, so young that her features had scarcely formed themselves, talking of the bitterest struggles of life, with the calm earnestness of one who had endured them all.[. . .]
>
> 'I go about the streets with water-creases, crying, "Four bunches a penny, water-creases." I am just eight years old – that's all, and I've a big sister, and a brother, and a sister younger than I am. On and off, I've been very near a twelvemonth in the streets. Before that, I had to take care of a baby for my aunt. No, it wasn't heavy – it was only two months old; but I minded it for ever such a time – till it could walk.[. . .] Before I had the baby, I used to help mother, who was in the fur trade; and if there were any slits in the fur, I'd sew them up. My mother learned me to needle-work and to knit when I was about five. I used to go to school, too, but I wasn't there long. I've forgot all about it now, it's such a time ago; and mother took me away because the master whacked me.[. . .]'

Mayhew's Watercress Girl is a useful reminder that childhood is at least as much a social construct as a physical stage, and accordingly that without an established concept of childhood, there can be no children's literature. It is undoubtedly for this reason, and not simply because of lack of time and education, that no working-class tradition of children's literature had evolved by the end of the nineteenth century, while by contrast, the late-Victorian and Edwardian bourgeoisie was busy creating a lively and prosperous children's publishing industry. Apart from the material distributed to them by religious and other organizations (usually in the form of tedious moral tracts), the children of the poor heard their stories in a very traditional way: by listening to the tales told by adults to pass the time as they worked, or in brief periods of leisure. These stories provided entertainment for all ages, and were rarely adapted for young listeners. Perhaps paradoxically, it was this working-class tradition of oral story-telling which was to inspire some of the most gifted writers of the Victorian period, and which kept alive tales of the imagination throughout the long dry period when educationists firmly believed that books for children should abjure fantasy and contain only useful information. This attitude was epitomized by the work of Maria Edgeworth whose *The Parents' Assistant* (1796) was widely read throughout the nineteenth century and influenced many of the *fin de siècle* and early twentieth-century writers for children. In her Preface to this work Edgeworth rebukes Doctor Johnson for his observation that young people prefer tales of 'giants and fairies, and castles and inchantments' (sic):

> The fact remains to be proved: but supposing they do prefer such tales, is this a reason why they should be indulged in reading them? It may be said that a little experience in life would soon convince them, that fairies, and giants, and enchanters, are not to be met with in the world. But why should the mind be filled with fantasie visions, instead of useful knowledge? Why should so much valuable time be lost? Why should we vitiate their taste, and spoil their appetite, by suffering them to feed upon sweetmeats?

Although Edgeworth's work was popular and influential, her antipathy to fairy tales and fantasy was outmoded well before the turn of the century, and in its closing years many distinguished writers and illustrators turned their hands to works of fantasy. Perhaps the best known of these were Andrew Lang, whose colour fairy books began to appear in 1889, and Oscar Wilde, whose two collections of fairy tales, *The Happy Prince and other tales* and *A House of Pomegranates*, were published in 1888 and 1891 respectively.

Lang's collections of fairy tales span the entire *fin de siècle* period; the first, *The Blue Fairy Book*, appearing in 1889, and the final volume, *The Lilac Fairy Book*, in 1910. Like his predecessors, the brothers Grimm, Andrew Lang was first and foremost a scholar. Indeed, his study of folk/fairy tales and myths led him to anticipate early anthropological studies such as Sir James Frazer's *The Golden Bough* (1926-36), and systems of analysis and classification such as that devised by the Russian intellectual, Vladimir Propp (whose *The Morphology of the Folk Tale*, 1923, is regarded as a precursor of Structuralism). Through his tireless and methodical collecting of tales from many cultures, Lang was able to show that there were structural relationships between tales which defied linguistic explanations. Lang argued that this underlined the innate importance of the tales, and he demonstrated his point by showing that they were not debased or popularized versions of more elaborate literary mythologies, but were in fact the origins of these more sophisticated works (see *Custom and Myth*, 1884; *Myth, Ritual and Religion*, 1899).

Andrew Lang also tried his hand at writing original fairy tales, including some specifically for children (notably *Prince Prigio*, 1889, and *Prince Ricardo of Pantouflia*, 1893), but their popularity has not survived. By contrast, the impresario of Decadence and Prince of the Aesthetes, Oscar Wilde, succeeded in inventing a selection of tales which have endured, some of them indeed becoming classics of the twentieth-century *fin de siècle*.

In the famous Preface to *The Picture of Dorian Gray*, Wilde proclaimed that a work of art should have no moral or political purpose. How far he abides by his own dictum in that novel is debatable; certainly in his fairy tales he largely rejects this principle. The majority of his fairy tales convey Wilde's world view very clearly. They question the morality of class divisions in society; specifically they condemn the parasitical nature of the ruling class and set up pointed contrasts between Christian values and the values of the socially powerful. The uncomfortable relationship between the sexes – and particularly the classist, sybaritic and coquettish behaviour associated with the wooing and marriage patterns of the ruling class – is also forcefully conveyed. Look, for instance, at the treatment of this subject in *The Happy Prince*. Before he encounters the gilded statue and learns the meaning of helping others, the sparrow has been caught up in a phantom romance with a 'most beautiful Reed':

'It is a ridiculous attachment,' twittered the other Swallows; 'she has no money and far too many relations;' and indeed the river was quite full of Reeds . . . After they had gone he began to tire of his lady-love. 'She has no conversation,' he said, 'and I am afraid that she is a coquette, for she is always flirting with the wind.' And certainly, whenever the wind blew, the Reed made the most graceful curtseys. (Complete Works of Oscar Wilde, p. 285)

Thus, in writing which was intended to include children in its audience, even Oscar Wilde felt it necessary to provide instruction, and to write for and about the ideal (who, like Christ, was to redeem the world) rather than the real child. The centrality of the childish ideal to Wilde's work is nowhere more clear than in his most famous and successful story, The Selfish Giant. This story borrows motifs and metaphors from a number of fairy tales and legends. It tells of an immensely rich giant who bans children from playing in his garden where, as a consequence, it is always winter. A young boy, who on one level at least is intended to stand for the Christ child, is helped by the Giant; accordingly the Giant is allowed to enter Paradise and the garden is brought back to life for the children who remain on earth.

The elevation of childhood typified by these stories is charac-teristic of a widespread tendency to look backwards rather than forwards at the end of the last century. This tendency was not unique to writing for or about childhood, but manifested itself in a variety of ways throughout the last century, many of them post-Darwinian attempts to understand human development as organic and evolutionary rather than divinely determined. The search for a Golden Age had also preoccupied a number of artists and writers, among them Ruskin, Pater, William Morris and the Pre-Raphaelites. Many of them thought of the past generally as superior to the present, and since childhood could be understood to represent the past in a number of ways (for instance, in the past all adults were children, children were thought to be more primitive than adults and so more closely linked to the past, etc.), it came to have considerable metaphoric value in late-Victorian Britain. As the children's book market flourished, a number of artists became involved in illustrating books for children, and they too seemed to be attracted to the past. Two well-known figures in the field of children's literature who exemplify this dual fascination with childhood and the past are Kenneth Grahame

WISHES.

Oh, if you were a little boy,
    And I was a little girl—
Why you would have some whiskers grow
    And then my hair would curl.

Ah! if I could have whiskers grow,
    I'd let you have my curls;
But what's the use of wishing it—
    Boys never can be girls.

An example of Kate Greenaway's 'body-less' idealized image of childhood. Compare this to Hoffman's 1844 illustration for *Struwwelpeter* (p.7), which deals only too clearly with real childhood and childish faults.

(1859–1932) (see his *The Golden Age*, 1895, and *Dream Days*, 1898) and Kate Greenaway (1846–1901).

Both Grahame and Greenaway are clearly concerned with adult perceptions of childhood, and though they place the child at the centre of their work and celebrate the period of childhood, their stories, poems, and pictures always provide comfortable fantasy images of ideal children. Greenaway's children in particular lack reality. Dressed in clothing modelled loosely on the fashions of the eighteenth century, they behave politely and prettily, and under their garments seem to have no bodies at all. This may be explained by her habit of using lay-figures (a jointed wooden manikin) rather than real children for models, but can also be understood as symptomatic of the way real children and real children's bodies were made to disappear in children's literature and were replaced by more spiritualized, ethereal, and idealized images (a useful comparison can be made between strategies for representing women in this period; see H. Michie's discussion of women in Victorian literature[19]). This lack of real bodies and their physical threat is a symptom of the growing need for adults to have a myth of childhood which is unthreatening and un-disturbing. Jacqueline Rose writes interestingly about this phenomenon in *The Case of Peter Pan, or, The Impossibility of Children's Fiction* (1984), where she identifies the kinds of para-doxical situations which may arise as a consequence of the adult construction of the childish ideal. Rose bases her 'case' on J. M. Barrie's *Peter Pan*, a text which in one form or another has been in the juvenile canon since it first appeared on stage in 1904, but which in fact was not originally written *for* children at all. The story of the boy who won't grow up first appeared in one of Barrie's adult novels, *The Little White Bird* (1902). It is told by the narrator, a bachelor who longs to have for his own the son of a couple he has befriended. He woos the baby boy with stories about Peter Pan, and at one point actually kidnaps him. As Rose points out, the man's desire for the boy, which is at the heart of this tale and which is retained in a variety of ways in many of the versions of *Peter Pan* which exist today, represents much that is frightening and even reprehensible to parents. However, since it first appeared in book form it has consistently been popular with grown-ups, and Rose's study tries to get to the heart of this contradiction. Essentially what she concludes is that the idealized image of

23

childhood which found its apotheosis in the *fin de siècle* is so powerful that the ambiguities which characterize the book (which may conceal issues such as homoerotic or paedophilic desire, a subject many would regard as inappropriate for children's literature) are not recognized.

The image of childhood represented by *Peter Pan* is a fantasy, and as *The Case of Peter Pan* points out, it is at the level of fantasy that sexuality is most active. Thus, one of the questions it is important to ask when reading fantasies written by adults for children is, 'What is this saying about sexuality?' Focusing on sexuality brings to the fore a surprising range of issues which previously may have seemed irrelevant to texts and genres. Look, for example, at one of the most popular areas of writing for young readers at the end of the last century – the adventure tale.

A great deal of work has been done on the attitudes to nation, race, class and gender characteristic of this genre, but most of the conclusions which have been reached are not unexpected. For instance, at a time when Britain's wealth and power were largely derived from her colonies but this imperial pre-eminence was under threat, it is not surprising to find writers applauding the virtues of empire and the exploits of the men who were responsible for expanding and controlling British territories. Similarly, when national pride and success depended on cheap labour and imported materials from the colonies, it would be surprising indeed if the literature written for the next generation of colonial administrators was concerned with the representation of the native populations or the morality of exploitative trading relationships. However, at a time when the childish ideal was largely characterized by sexual innocence, it might be surprising to discover that a great deal of the most widely read and popular children's literature can be read as exploring the erotic fantasies and sexual discontents of its authors. In fact, as became apparent in the discussion of *Peter Pan*, it seems to be precisely *because* childhood is presumed to be innocent that so many writers have felt it safe to let their private fantasies find expression in writing for children. Consciously or unconsciously, children's literature has often been treated as a safe-house, and this is particularly true of the literature written during and shortly after the *fin de siècle*.

Looking specifically at attitudes to women and the conventions of heterosexual romance, it is possible to see that these have been explored in a variety of ways in adventure fiction. For instance, Peter Brooks has pointed to the processes of sublimation at work in much adventure writing for young readers as evidenced precisely by the absence of women. He asks why so much adventure fiction – which may also include domestic adventures such as *Winnie the Pooh* and *The Wind in the Willows* – celebrates all-male environments and the bachelor life, and concludes:

> The world of the adventure novel is essentially pre-pubescent, one where antagonism, confrontations, lure, excitement do not demand, may even explicitly interdict the presence of women. The interdiction can be read as a sublimation. If one were to analyze the kind of joyous fear evoked by Stevenson's *Treasure Island* – surely one of the masterpieces of womanless fiction – its progressive creation of mystery and suspense, its movement out from the home across the sea to the island, to nightmare and to treasure, one could probably trace the perfect adequation of this tale of adventure to the erotic pursuit . . . By the conventions of the adventure tale, all problematical psychological issues are sublimated to the overt gesture of man in intelligent, controlled, and eventually successful conflict with the mysterious and daemonic forces of his environment – forces which in adult literature will tend to concentrate on the erotic daemon.[20]

Brooks is suggesting that the reason women are so often absent in adventure fiction is because the text is dealing with issues which cannot be spoken about. This idea takes us back to Rose's recognition that sexuality and fantasy are tightly interlaced, and central to the formation of the self. Because of this, both are seminal concerns of the psychoanalyst, and it is perhaps as an analogue of the patient-analyst relationship that the treatment of sexuality in juvenile adventure fiction is best understood. Psychoanalysis is about interpretation: interpreting what is meant through what the patient is able to say, for at the heart of the process is the paradox that the patient is attempting to talk about things which – for many reasons – s/he is unable to say. Similarly, the writer of adventure fiction can be understoood to be disguising, more or less effectively, what s/he needs to say behind what can be said. At the end of the last century the vocabulary for talking about the unconscious was rudimentary, but even had it existed, in an age when talking personally about sex was taboo, covert ways of dealing with the problems, anxieties, tensions, and satisfactions it aroused had to be found. This is particularly true when there was a mismatch between social expectation and individual desire. This mismatch seems to unite a large number of prominent writers for children; especially male writers of the late-Victorian and Edwardian period.

The implied desire of man for boy in *Peter Pan* has already been discussed; a closely related motif runs through many other well-known children's books – the rejection of women. Biographies of writers such as Kenneth Grahame and A. A. Milne provide considerable evidence to support the idea that Victorian/ Edwardian parenting patterns could lead to problematic relations between the sexes. One of the most convincing readings of both *The Wind in the Willows* and the Pooh stories is provided by Humphrey Carpenter in *Secret Gardens* (London, 1985). Carpenter stresses the problems both writers had in being married, their preference for all-male environments such as their private clubs, their difficulty in relating to their children, and their unhappiness that it was their writing for children which made them famous. Behind both writers' work is the same fear of growing up and finding a place in the adult world, which Barrie captured so brilliantly in *Peter Pan*. In *The Wind in the Willows* and *Winnie the Pooh* we see Grahame and Milne attempting to capture and preserve childhood – not for generations of children to come, but for themselves (both, by all accounts, enjoyed their time as children enormously). In writing about idyllic childhood it was made safe and able to be revisited whenever it was needed – a constant escape from the dreary realities of grown-up existence. This is the reassuring, if rather twee, note struck at the end of *The House at Pooh Corner*: 'wherever they go, and whatever happens to them on the way, in that enchanted place on the top of the Forest a little boy and his Bear will always be playing' (p. 178).

Although the guarantee that the Hundred Acre Wood will be forever present takes the form of a promise, according to Humphrey Carpenter this final scene was at one level Milne's attempt to kill off Pooh and all his friends and so free himself of the label 'author of *Winnie the Pooh*'. Like so many writers – and particularly *male* writers – A. A. Milne regarded writing for children as an incidental sideline to his 'real' work, writing for adults. He felt diminished and disregarded by the literary establishment because of the success of his children's *oeuvre*. This attitude has bedevilled children's literature for most of this century, and has contributed to the stylistic conservatism which has, until recently, dominated writing for children.

STYLE AND STATUS IN CHILDREN'S LITERATURE

The stylistic conservatism of children's literature seems to have been a consequence of two related factors. First was the splitting out of children's literature from the mainstream of family fiction, making of it a new and distinct genre. This separation was brought about through the conjunction of a variety of factors. Undoubtedly one of the most important of these was the impetus which came with the advent of universal, compulsory education in 1880. Children were now not only thought of as readers, but they were also separated from the adult population more clearly than ever before. Governmental legislation which required young people to attend school between the ages of 5 and 14 effectively created a physical stage of childhood which had not existed when children were expected to start contributing to the family income as soon as they were physically able to (often as early as 4 or 5 years of age). Whether they wanted it or not (and in the 1890s many working-class children – especially boys – found their enforced attendance at school financially punitive and socially demeaning), the majority of children had their childhoods extended and forever changed by the requirement to attend school.

As childhood became a more distinct phase, it was understood to have its own reading needs and requirements. Perhaps perversely, concern about what was suitable and useful for children was instrumental in the process of relegating children's literature to the bottom of the literary hierarchy. 'Suitable for children' came for many to be synonymous with anodyne and stylistically moribund. Among other factors, this resulted in the conscious exclusion of children from the audience for 'serious' fiction.[21] The corollary to this was, as typified by Barrie, Grahame, and Milne, that writers who took themselves seriously were unhappy to be thought of as 'children's authors'. While in many ways the result of this separation of adult and juvenile writing could be said to have been a form of brake on the kind of work which could be written for young readers, especially at the end of the last century it also opened up new opportunities for one body of writers. In writing for children many women were able to forge careers, and some found themselves able to address topical and controversial issues and attitudes in acceptable ways.

WOMEN WRITERS FOR CHILDREN

Over the years many theories have been put forward as to why women came to represent the largest body of writers for children by the end of the last century. For instance, it has been argued that women found it easy to write for children because women were used to being with children; particularly in their roles as mothers, governesses, Sunday-school teachers, and so on. Related to this body of opinion is the idea that women could write for children because intellectually and emotionally women were like children. A less derogatory thesis to explain why women may have been attracted to writing for children is that because children's literature was regarded as less serious and significant than literature for adults, it was seen as a respectable way for women to earn money, whereas most forms of employment, including writing for adults, were not. While there is undoubtedly truth in most of these arguments, the most interesting work I know on the relationship between women writers and children's literature is put forward by Julia Briggs in 'Women Writers and Writing for Children'.[22] Briggs begins her study with the work of the eighteenth-century writer, Sarah Fielding (inevitably known as the sister of her more famous brother, Henry), and ends with the turn-of-the century writer E. Nesbit. Her study argues convincingly that there is a marked shift in the kind of writing women produce for children in the century and a half which separates these two writers. Women like Sarah Fielding began by wanting to prove that they were serious writers and thinkers. Accordingly, they tried to demonstrate their understanding of traditionally male subjects such as theology, history, philosophy, the natural sciences, literature, and educational debates. Their writing was designed to promote and reproduce the values espoused by the male academic and social establishment. Their efforts were largely ignored – as women and writers for children they were simply doubly marginalized. Gradually, Briggs argues, a new trend developed. This was for women to see their situation and cause as being analogous to children's: both groups were disparaged and repressed by the prevailing social order. As this idea took hold, it seems that some women were able to use children's literature to poke fun at the male establishment; no longer were they attempting to reproduce male values and attitudes, rather they began to challenge and subvert it. While a number of the best-known women writers for children are shown to have been subversive in a variety of ways (in the same collection of essays Humphrey Carpenter looks at Beatrix Potter's 'impertinent' and subversive bunnies), this technique reaches its apotheosis in the work of E. Nesbit.

Nesbit (1858–1924) had written stories, books, and articles for a number of years before she established her reputation as a writer for children. The secret of her success was that she rejected once and for all the overtly adult voice of most narrators and adopted the voice of the child – often using one of her child characters to narrate her texts. As Henry James had already shown in *What Maisie Knew*, adopting the child's voice and/or point of view does not necessarily mean becoming infantile. Rather, often through the disparity between the innocence of the child and what s/he reports or observes, parody, satire, and social critique can be made particularly effectively. Nesbit was an unorthodox character; for instance, she was a Fabian socialist who had short hair and smoked at a time when both were thought shockingly unfeminine. However, she depended on the income from her writing to support her family and, as a consequence, in her earlier work she tended to express the kinds of ideas in the kinds of ways she thought would be acceptable to publishers and the majority of the reading public. When she began to specialize in children's literature and adopt the child's point of view, however, she found herself able to be more radical in tone, content, and style. Julia Briggs describes the advantages of writing for children to Nesbit as a woman writer:

> In adopting the voice of the child, in exposing the adult world to the child's critical gaze, E. Nesbit had, ironically, found a way of articulating her feelings of rebelliousness and subversiveness as a woman. Adopting the child's voice allowed her not only to locate her own position as a woman in a male-dominated society, but also to escape from the pressure to write like a man.[23]

While E. Nesbit and a handful of distinguished women writers may have been using children's literature to articulate their views on the need to change the role of women in society, an equally influential body of work was emphasizing the need to uphold traditional sexual stereotypes and maintain differences between the sexes.

CLASS, GENDER, AND CHILDREN'S LITERATURE

We now take it as natural that some books are clearly intended for an audience of boys, while others appeal specifically to girl readers, but this was not always the case. In the early and middle years of the nineteenth century most children's literature was intended to be read by both boys and girls (think of *The Fairchild Family*). By the end of the century, however, there began to be increased anxiety about what was happening to the familiar patterns of manly and womanly behaviour. On the one hand, women were agitating for social and legal reforms which would give them more independence; on the other, men were struggling in their attempts to govern the country and rule the empire effectively. Children's literature was one of the most obvious and influential ways of reaching the next generation and trying to correct what seemed to be failings in the way understanding about appropriate behaviour for both sexes was being transmitted. The result was that images of masculinity and femininity in children's books began to be more exaggerated, and books began to be written and marketed with gender very much in mind.

For boys, changes in the content of their fiction were matched by changes in what it was thought appropriate for them to read. At the level of content, the change can be demonstrated very effectively by comparing two stories about life at a boys' school: Frederick Farrar's *Eric, or Little by Little* (1858) and Rudyard Kipling's *Stalky & Co.* (1899). In the middle years of the century, masculinity was a relatively open construct. The ideal boy was Christian, dutiful, self-sacrificing, and not ashamed of showing his emotions, as can be seen in the following passage from *Eric* in which Eric is visiting his friend, Edward Russell, who is in the process of dying following an accident while out with Eric. Eric has brought some primroses for the invalid:

Russell was pressing the flowers to his lips. 'The grass withereth,' he murmured, 'the flower fadeth, and the glory of his beauty perisheth; but – *but* the word of the Lord endureth for ever.' And here he too burst into natural tears, and Eric pressed his hand with more than a brother's fondness to his heart.

'Oh, Eddy, Eddy, my heart is full,' he said, 'too full to speak to you. Let me read to you;' and with Russell's arm around his neck, he sat down beside his pillow, and read to him . . . At first sobs choked his voice, but it gathered firmness as he went on. (p. 147)

Attributes of masculinity which were perfectly acceptable in 1858 – such things as crying, hugging, expressing love rather than comradeship – had by the *fin de siècle* been banished to the realm of the feminine. Indeed, Farrar's text is explicitly ridiculed by the three central character's in Kipling's book. While Eric fights a losing battle with his conscience, Beetle, Stalky, and M'Turk declare war on and conquer foes of every age and class and seem to ignore their consciences entirely. Farrar's concern is that boys be shown how to grow up to be Christian gentlemen; the project of *Stalky* is to show that the kind of men who can successfully expand and rule the empire need to live on their wits and physical daring rather than their precarious sense of morality.

In addition to limiting and hardening acceptable forms of masculinity, changes in writing for boys were also involved with the general nature of boys' reading. Future defenders of the empire needed to be masters of fact, highly rational, independent, and completely in charge of their emotions. Clearly fiction, with its interest in relationships and the inner life, was of less use in creating the right kind of boy than was non-fiction. Accordingly, boys were steered away from novels (with the exception of the highly patriotic and masterful adventure stories of the day) and towards informative publications. Their magazines taught them how to make things, how to carry out scientific experiments, how to stuff animals, what flags of the world looked like, how heroes won battles, how athletes trained, and generally attempted to instil in them what was thought to be a manly set of codes and values. By contrast, girls' novels and publications tried equally hard to teach girls how to become feminine.

While boys were steered away from reading fiction, reading novels came to be seen as a very acceptable way for a young lady to spend her time. Indeed, one of the most interesting aspects of the hardening of sexual stereotypes which occurs in *fin de siècle* children's literature is that whereas previously girls' reading had been viewed with suspicion because it was thought that girls who read were in danger of developing their brains at the expense of the rest of their bodies (thereby unfitting them for childbearing), or that reading would introduce them to dangerously unfeminine knowledge or distract them from their domestic duties, by the 1890s girls' reading was no longer perceived as problematic. The reason for this seems to be that in the intervening years a form of literature specifically designed for girls had been invented, and was so successful in its ambition to maintain the sexual *status quo* that girls internalized its messages and ultimately turned everything they read into confirmation of it.

A good example of the sleight of hand by which girls' fiction seemed to be responding to the modern world but was actually reasserting traditional values is provided by the girls' school story, which came to prominence in Britain with the work of L. T. Meade (1854–1914). Meade was one of the most prolific and popular writers of her day. Her school stories demonstrate very effectively the ambivalence surrounding higher education for women and the way children's literature was developing into a conservative – even reactionary – genre. *A Sweet Girl Graduate* (1897) is particularly interesting. It tells the story of Priscilla, a clever young woman who, as a consequence of being orphaned, is sent to a women's college to be educated so that she can support her many siblings. Because of her financial exigency, Priscilla's desire to be educated is not seen as unfeminine. However, she turns out to be a brilliant scholar and likely to get a First Class classics degree – and studying the classics was *not* considered feminine as it could expose girls to material which was sexually dubious. Meade drives this point home by increasing the family's financial problems so that as she nears the end of her course Priscilla realizes that she needs to abandon her ambition and to concentrate on modern languages – a more useful field of study for a future governess.

It might be supposed that her Principal, as head of one of the new and contentious women's colleges, would be a proto-feminist and object to this sacrifice. Instead, she applauds Priscilla's decision, explaining that her action will win a crown of gold more valuable than the crown of bay she might have gained through her intellectual ability.

A Sweet Girl Graduate shows how *fin de siècle* girls' fiction reconciled changes in life-style and opportunities for girls with a conservative definition of femininity. The rapid changes in girls' lives gave rise to a literature which encouraged its readers to believe that they could move with the times and could modify their behaviour without departing from traditional expectations. More importantly, reformed characters like Priscilla, who were seen to abandon their unorthodox ambitions, worked as role models who encouraged girl readers to react against change, collude in their own containment, and uphold a moral ambience based on feminine idealism.

Because reading is an essentially private experience, and one which is bound up in language, it is instrumental in shaping how children perceive the world and themselves within it. Consequently, the importance of the separation of children's literature on the basis of gender has had profound and lasting implications, although the reasons which initially lay behind it are no longer relevant at the end of the twentieth century. Indeed, one of the major social concerns of this *fin de siècle* is with ensuring equal opportunities between the sexes, but this goal is constantly hindered by obsolete gender roles conveyed by much children's literature, and by the social conditions which continue to create girls who read predominantly fiction, and boys who, when they read at all, tend to read non-fiction. While their reading lives diverge so early, with boys being discouraged from reading fiction as part of the process of making them autonomous and socially powerful (but possibly at the expense of their emotional development and affective relationships), and girls being guided towards fiction of a kind which seems to justify passivity, resignation, self-sacrifice and self-regulation, shared experiences and perceptions – necessary for both to have equal opportunities in the many different spheres of modern life – may be seriously hindered.

However dubious the consequences may appear today, in publishing terms the initial decision to create separate literatures for boys and girls proved very successful. By the turn of the century it was a well-established part of publishing practice, and as a consequence reproduced itself over the decades. Certainly there remained a mainstream of juvenile fiction which appealed equally to both sexes and there continued to be women writers who exploited the subversive potential of the genre (the rather

33

bohemian tales of female enterprise created by Noel Streatfeild are good examples), but for the most part the patterns of juvenile publishing were to remain unchanged until the closing decades of the twentieth century. The tenacity of these early developments reflects the continued adherence to the Victorian ideal of childhood, with its implied promises of redemption, security, and escape for adults, and its prospects of power and recognition for young readers. The intensity of these feelings was in part created by the fact that adulthood was not only inevitable, but, until the post-war period, achieved rapidly. As this century progressed, childhood was prolonged to include adolescence (and with it the new youth culture); gradually the Victorian ideal was eroded.

2

Growing Up Is
Hard To Do

POST-WAR CHILDHOOD AND CHILDREN'S LITERATURE

At the end of the nineteenth century the issues dealt with in children's literature were controlled by adults' images, needs and expectations of childhood. Accordingly, children in children's books were for the most part beautiful, innocent, and the source of every kind of salvation. This version of literary childhood persisted more or less unchallenged throughout the Edwardian period and between the wars, and for many of the same reasons. Where the adults of the *fin de siècle* felt anxious about the changing world and reluctant to face its possible demands, adults living between the wars also required that their image of childhood provide a sense of hope, purpose, cleansing and continuity to alleviate the disruption and futility of war. The uncertainty of the future perpetuated the same need to return to origins and try to discover where things had gone wrong which had been preoccupying children's writers for the previous half-century. Accordingly, the most remarkable developments in juvenile fiction came in the period following the Second World War.

This post-war period reflected a number of social pressures. Of most interest here are its responses to the family, to gender, and perhaps pre-eminently, to the sense of living in a post-atomic age (the incorporation of the new youth culture of the 1950s is conspicuously absent from writing for children and young adults in this period – and for a long time to come). Within the confines of this study it is not possible to discuss in detail the range of children's books produced at this time, but close examination of three representative texts from this period provides a good picture of the dominant trends in juvenile fiction and the ideology underpinning them. The texts I have selected are Mary Norton's *The Borrowers* (1952), Lucy M. Boston's *The Children of Green Knowe* (1954), and Philippa Pearce's *Tom's Midnight Garden* (1958). Readers wishing to know more about the children's literature of this period will find some interesting discussions of other texts in Margaret and Michael Rustin's *Narratives of Love and Loss* (London, 1987).

UNHAPPY FAMILIES

There developed in the sixties a radical critique of the family. The anti-psychiatry movement, associated especially with R. D. Laing, saw the family as a source of mental illness – in particular, schizophrenia. Even more fundamental, at the end of the period, was the sexual politics of the women's and gay movements. The family's narrow channelling of sexuality, its socializing of children into rigid gender roles and its oppression of women in the domestic roles of wife and mother – these were just some of the criticisms. The common ground was an analysis of the family as incorporating in its very structure – and thus perpetuating – the negative elements of society at large.[1]

Although all three books were written within six years of one another, they demonstrate the rapidity with which ideas about the family and its place in society were being redefined – and of course within this new definition an altered understanding of childhood was included. Chronologically earliest, *The Borrowers* is also the text which is most obviously concerned with trying to reconcile pre- and post-war images of childhood. The boy who is to change the Clock family's life belongs to the pre-war world of upper- and middle-class Britain. Like so many children of his class, the boy was born in India but sent home to England to be educated. His is a story which emphasizes the problems of separation endured by generations of British boys, and made more acute when the trials of boarding school were compounded by huge geographical distances. Holidays, or in his case con-valescence, were rarely spent with families, but required that children be sent away to friends or relatives, or professionally cared for.

While the pattern is familiar, Mary Norton carefully blurs the edges of the boy's story – details of time, place and duration are kept to a minimum – which means that the boy's separation from his family can be read metaphorically. On one level it is the old story of childhood loneliness caused by social practice; on the other, it is an almost archetypal expression of anxiety about lost families and social chaos. No longer is the pattern of life, including periodic reunions with family, predictable. In the post-war period many families were still recovering from the traumas of loss and separation caused by war. As far as children were concerned, the widespread disruption to family life caused by the policy of evacuating children from urban centres was an entirely new and cross-class experience which was often profoundly disturbing. Added to this were the problems caused by food shortages, rationing, and the sporadic and chaotic removals caused by bomb damage, all of which are conveyed in the story of the Borrowers. Though once part of a thriving and stable community, the Clocks now live a meagre existence and no longer know where to find their family and friends.

The boy is not the only child in the story. His relationship with Arrietty, the youngest Borrower, is what brings about the action of the story. The boy lives in a malign adult world full of irrational anger (Mrs Driver), benign irresponsibility (Great Aunt Sophy) and institutionalized murder (represented by the ratcatcher, with his terriers and gas, though clearly Aunt Sophy is also linked to the force of destruction which invades her house as her initials form the word 'gas'). He is alternately neglected and abused. By contrast, Arrietty is over-protected. Unlike the boy, she is better educated than her parents (another gesture towards the social changes taking place in post-war Britain and which were resulting in divisions in families), and ambitious. The Clock parents are traditionalists. They want to maintain the old social order, including its reliable divisions based on class and gender (though occasionally Homily criticizes those, like the Overmantles, who think themselves superior on the basis of material possessions). Circumstances demand change, however, and Arrietty is allowed to do things no female Borrower has ever done before. The problems and tensions which result from her actions are portrayed as both liberating and potentially dangerous – they lead to the devastating destruction of the Clock household and the attempt to exterminate the family, but also bring about the end of the family's moribund and isolated existence. The upheaval may signal the beginning of the end, but it may also represent the dawning of a new and better life.

The significance of the Clock family's exodus is marked by the fact that the old grandfather clock in the old house deep in an old and quiet bit of the country stops. Thinking back to the pre-war preoccupation with time and the desire to halt progress suggests one way of reading this, but it is also possible to understand it as symbolizing the break in continuity brought about by the wars, and especially the threat represented by the atom bomb. Not only had technology and social change advanced so far and so fast that it was inconceivable that the old world could be recovered (and many had begun to regard the pre-war era as a Golden Age), but there now existed the means of stopping time permanently through the mass destruction of life on the planet.

The guilt, fear and uncertainty of the post-atomic age are central concerns in the Green Knowe books of Lucy M. Boston.[2] The desire to bridge the abyss between past and present and so heal some of the psychic and social wounds she felt were damaging society takes a number of forms in *The Children of Green Knowe*. The story begins with Tolly's arrival at Green Knowe, which, like the house in *The Borrowers*, is an ancient country manor. To get there Tolly has to cross the flooded river, and in his dreams that night he recognizes that the old house is like Noah's Ark, as he tells Granny Oldknow, who replies:

> 'Yes, all the children used to call it the Ark. Your grandfather did, and he learnt it from his father, who learnt it from his, and so on, right the way back. But you called it that by yourself.' (p. 22)

The resemblance to the Ark is strengthened as the story progresses and it becomes clear that the house, and Granny Oldknow, belong not to any one time but to all time. Generations co-exist at Green Knowe (an important part of the plot involves Tolly's making friends with his ghostly ancestors and accommodating their pasts into his present), which is a place of healing. At Green Knowe Tolly learns about the past, but he also learns to live in harmony with the natural world and to appreciate the powers of the creative imagination. He begins to dream, and in his dreams finds links to his everyday life. Structurally, Tolly's dreams are paralleled with stories from the past told to him by

Granny Oldknow, and gradually Tolly (and the reader) begin to see the links between the stories, the dreams, and the real world of Green Knowe. Thus the kind of healing that Tolly experiences is both personal and metaphoric.

On the personal level, Tolly's needs are very like those of the boy in *The Borrowers*. This is another story of a displaced child – his mother has died, and his recently remarried father is living in Burma. He is unhappy at his boarding school, and frightened of spending his holidays with an old relative he has never met. Unlike Mary Norton's boy, however, Tolly finds at Green Knowe an adult world which welcomes and supports him. The differences between their experiences can perhaps best be understood by comparing their attitudes to the houses they visit. Very often houses are used to symbolize the psyche. A huge, dark, cold house such as Aunt Sophy's, with many unexplored rooms to which entry is forbidden, effectively mirrors the fear and repression felt by the child. In *The Borrowers*, the boy finds a tiny space which he is able to inhabit, and significantly he populates it with the kind of loving family from which he is excluded. The home under the floorboards can be understood to be his fantasy world which sustains the qualities of love, relationships, femininity and imagination which are largely denied in his present reality. Significantly, when he leaves Aunt Sophy it is to go on a voyage with his sisters back to their home.

Tolly's experiences at Green Knowe are very different. While Norton's boy in many ways seems to regress, Tolly begins to grow up and to expand. He explores the whole of the house and its grounds; he learns its history, and in the process becomes more confident of himself and able to function in the world. Perhaps most important of all for the purposes of this discussion, whereas the boy in *The Borrowers* never makes any satisfactory links with the adult world, Tolly learns to see the relationships between past and present, which makes him understand that inside all the adults he meets are the children they were, and inside himself is the adult he will be. The sense of discontinuity which typified the post-war period and found its best-known expression in adolescent culture (music, dance, fashion, films, all of which rejected adults and adult values) is systematically combated in *The Children of Green Knowe*. With her interest in the collective unconscious and her determination to foreground continuity and coherence, Boston essentially brings the 'Beautiful Child' into the present day.

Many of the themes and issues characteristic of Norton's and Boston's novels are also found in *Tom's Midnight Garden*: the isolated pre-pubescent boy in the large house; the disruption of linear time (Tom always enters the garden when the clock strikes thirteen); the exploration of the relationship between child and adult; anxiety about the effects of change on the landscape; and perhaps as important as any of these qualities, the mutual affection and dependence of male and female characters. In different ways each of these writers emphasizes the unnatural nature of gender-specific behaviour. As part of the process of growing up and becoming independent, the boys are made to acknowledge and accept the feminine parts of themselves as they appear in their female companions. This is an interesting development, as independence in boys is usually thought to involve denying many of the feminine aspects of the self, and especially the capacity to nurture and develop affective relationships.[3] Looking back to Jonathan Dollimore's assessment of changing attitudes to the family in the 1960s, it seems that already in juvenile fiction the problems he describes – especially rigid socializing and adherence to strict gender roles – are being anticipated and countered. Unfortunately, the relative lack of boy readers, itself a product of such socialization, made such thoughtful texts less powerful than they might have been.

CONTEMPORARY FANTASY AND CHILDHOOD

Each of the three texts discussed reveals a continued preoccupation with the child as inheritor of a fallen world which s/he is capable of (at least partially) saving, healing and restoring. Despite the fact that all were written during a period when the family was central to social policy and media images,[4] each concentrates on the activities of a single (male) child, cut off from family and friends, and his efforts to make a bridge between the modern world and the past (even in books where siblings are present, such as C. S. Lewis's Narnia chronicles (1950-6), the children have been separated from their home and parents because of the war). These books are typical of the trend which dominated both pre- and post-war fiction for children: the use of a fantasy world to make comments about the present state of civilization. Additionally, by the 1950s, understanding of the psyche and the importance of childhood for the development of healthy individuals (and so, collectively, of healthy societies) provided a further, conscious, dimension to fantasy writing for children. Whereas in the past writers such as J. M. Barrie and Lewis Carroll seem, perhaps unwittingly, to have used fantasy journeys as ways of exploring their own needs and fear of adult responsibilities, now writers began to explore the potential of fantasy to deal with the kinds of problems children inevitably faced as part of the process of growing up: fear of separation, loss, sexuality, death, anger, and so on (indeed, the psychologist Bruno Bettelheim was later to argue in *The Uses of Enchantment* (1976) that these fears were effectively dealt with in one of the earliest and most basic forms of children's literature: fairy tales). The psychoanalysts Michael and Margaret Rustin discuss a range of twentieth-century texts from this perspective in *Narratives of Love and Loss*; however, the best example is curiously absent from their study. This is writer-psychiatrist Catherine Storr's *Marianne Dreams* (1958).

Marianne falls ill with an unspecified disease on her tenth birthday (significant because the double digit heralds adolescence). As the book develops, it becomes clear that Marianne's health is linked to her mental state: forced to stay in bed for weeks on end, her dream life takes on a new, vivid, and ultimately therapeutic role, subtly suggesting areas in her life which had been problematic. The book is never explicit about what troubles Marianne, though there are some hints. Approaching adolescence is one sub-text, but it is also apparent that Marianne has a distant relationship with her father and younger brother. Neither of these male figures features in her daily life until she begins to recover. They are, however, replaced by a different significant male who combines elements of both father and sibling. This is Mark, a boy who in Marianne's waking life is slowly recovering from polio and who is taught by the same home-tutor as Marianne. In Marianne's dream world Mark remains ill (Marianne is well here), but as the two are thrown together and have to give up their selfish and egotistical ways of behaving to escape from THEM, evil, peering, giant stone erections who want to crush them, both children's health begins to improve.

Marianne's dream world is set in a picture she draws at the beginning of her illness, before she knows that she will be confined to bed for many weeks. It is a typical child's drawing of a house – not as houses are, but as we learn to see them:

> A house with four windows and a front door. The walls were not quite straight, because she wasn't ruling the lines, and the chimney was a little large. Over the chimney she drew a faint scribble of smoke . . . She drew a fence around the house, and a path leading from the front door to a gate. She put some flowers inside the fence, and all around drew long scribbly grass, which she hoped would be waist high at least. In the grass outside the fence she drew a few large rough-looking stones or lumps of rock, like those she had seen on the moors in Cornwall. (p. 15)

It doesn't take a trained analyst to see that there are significant features of this early version of the house – especially when the description is read with the illustration which accompanies it. For Marianne's house is defended – the windows are small, and a fence keeps out the wild world of grass and stone. The chimney is large, but only a faint column of smoke comes from it so that it is not clear whether there is anybody inside tending the fire. No curtains or ornaments suggest that the house is inhabited, and the world beyond the house is unrestrained, though essentially natural. When Marianne reaches the house for the first time in her dream, another significant feature becomes apparent: there is no way to open the door.

The house reflects Marianne's moods. At first she begins to try to improve, and adds a doorknob and knocker as well as someone (Mark) at a window. When she gets in, she finds the house empty and cold. Gradually Marianne begins to fill the house with detail, and to develop her relationship with Mark (another of the male/female dyads, though in reverse this time). When they quarrel and she scribbles over the house she doesn't visit it for days. In her real world Mark (who is also Marianne's alter ego) gets terribly ill, and Marianne herself begins to decline. This time she deals contructively with her guilt and anxiety, and helps Mark to escape from the house and the crushing stones to a lighthouse by the sea which she furnishes and fills with good food for Mark. Now that she has learned to deal with her anger rather than to deny it or let it overwhelm her, Marianne begins to recover. At the same time it becomes apparent that she is no longer afraid of the world beyond her house, and no longer anxious about whether she is a child or an adult: the tower is in open space looking out to sea, and Marianne has filled it to capacity with a huge variety of objects, as Mark observes:

> 'If you put in any more we shan't be able to get up and downstairs. I've had to put the last lot of books on the steps as it is, since you drew in that model railway all round the walls. You know we really didn't need that.'
> 'No, but it's fun,' Marianne said, unrepentantly. (p. 190)

Yet for all Marianne's progress, the book has an ambiguous ending. Having got as far as the tower, the children realize that they want to go further – to the sea. The tower is still a resting place, and one cut off from the real world. When they resolve how and where to meet, Marianne's recovery in the real world seems complete, and she ceases dreaming. On the night before she leaves for a family holiday by the sea she makes one more trip to the tower to find that Mark has gone without her. At first Marianne is angry, but when she finds a note from Mark to say that he will come back in a helicopter to get her as soon as he can, Marianne lies down to wait for him.

This ending can be read in a variety of ways. To some it means that Mark (whose progress in the real world has never been as good as Marianne's) has died and that in lying down to wait for him Marianne is choosing death too. For others the ending is life-affirming. Marianne is content to wait because now she is confident in her relationship with Mark and is in no hurry to rush into its real-life romantic counterpart. In the recent cinematic adaptation of this text, *Paper House* (1988), both readings are explored. We are told that Mark has died, and when he returns in the helicopter and Marianne tries to reach him, she nearly falls off a cliff and kills herself. She is pulled back from the edge by her parents; as she turns to them Mark flies off without her.

In books such as *Marianne Dreams* a marked change in emphasis from earlier writing for children begins to emerge. While clearly the image of the child in the books and the understanding of what the child needs inevitably continues to be dictated by adults, there is a greater attempt to understand children's needs; to value fiction for young readers less for its ability to conceal adult fears and needs, and more for its ability to help its intended audience deal with the real and perceived problems and pressures they experience as part of the process of growing up. Paradoxically, it is precisely this interest in understanding and catering for the needs of children which has resulted in writing which often seems to foreclose on childhood. The refusal to grow up is no longer a dominant motif in juvenile fiction but has been replaced by writing which is specifically preoccupied with facilitating the maturing process.

In many ways, the current emphasis on writing which helps young people deal with the world in which they live (both psychologically and practically) can legitimately be compared to the didacticism which underlay much of the early writing for children discussed in part 1. But where writers such as Maria Edgeworth were primarily concerned with providing facts, information, and moral lessons, and their followers (for instance, Frances Hodgson Burnett and E. Nesbit) wrote stories which celebrated childhood and attempted to make their central characters better *children*, contemporary writers of realistic children's literature work from the premise that children and young adults experience the world as very complex and often difficult. Writers such as Aidan Chambers, Robert Cormier, Berlie Doherty, Alan Garner, Rosa Guy, Joan Lingard, and Robert Westall (to name a few) write about events and incidents which today's young people may encounter (directly or indirectly): such things as bullying, divorce, sexism, betrayal, sex and sexuality, mental or physical disability, adolescent instability, environmental issues, drugs, crime, rejection, death, and disease. Often these works are equally concerned with issues and events writers feel young readers ought to know about even if they are unlikely themselves to have experienced them. Sometimes these are general issues or social problems which will, of course, be real for many readers (for instance racism, bigotry, poverty, violence, sexual abuse, the threat of nuclear destruction, war, and death); other texts are more specific. For example, in 1992 Elizabeth Laird won the Book of the Year award (based on children's responses to texts) for *Kiss the Dust*, a novel about the problems experienced by the Kurds during the Iran-Iraq war; in 1993 the late Robert Westall was a finalist for the same award with his novella *Gulf*.

Gulf is typical of much contemporary writing for children in that it doesn't discount the young reader's ability to deal with difficult moral and social dilemmas, and also displays contemporary writers' preoccupation with conveying subjective experience. Like all of Westall's work, it is a difficult story to summarize, but at its simplest it is a 'mind-travel' story about a young English boy, Figgis, who is so affected by what he hears about the Gulf War (especially through the media) that he is taken over by the personality of an Iraqi soldier (also a boy). In the comfortable world of suburban England he begins to live out the life of the young soldier – a life which alternates between excruciating boredom and discomfort, and even more acute fear. The contrast between the two worlds is powerfully and economically made, and Westall carefully avoids taking sides: the reader is put in the position of sympathizing with both characters. When reading *Gulf* it is impossible not to understand that the wars which fill our television screens, radio reports, and newspapers are happening to ordinary people (many of them technically 'children') who could be us and who don't share our perceptions about who is 'right'.

At the end of *Gulf*, the protagonist is 'healed' in that he becomes an ordinary boy again (his obliviousness to the problems of the world is metaphorically condemning), and his childishness emphasized. However, his brother, who has been relating the events in the book, has been changed irrevocably: the experiences he has undergone have given him an adult's perspective of the world. The drive behind realistic children's fiction – to make childhood safe by preparing readers for the brutalities of the world – lies at the heart of the paradox described above. For, in attempting to protect children, writers often accelerate the pace at which children grow up. Certainly at the end of their stories (and an interesting comparison can be made between the closure characteristic of fantasy fiction and that associated with realistic writing for children), the protagonists have clearly left childhood behind. This pattern can be seen in a wide range of contemporary juvenile fiction. Some of the earliest and clearest examples are provided by Afro-American writers such as Rosa Guy and Mildred D. Taylor, whose historical series (beginning with *Roll of Thunder, Hear My Cry*, 1976) tells what it was like to grow up black in the American South. The book for which Rosa Guy is best known, *The Friends* (1973), tells the story of Phyllisia, a West Indian girl whose family moves to New York's Harlem district, where she suffers racist bullying at school, gets caught up in street fighting, loses her mother through breast cancer, and finally learns that she has been deluding herself about her family's wealth and status. As if this weren't enough, Phyl makes friends with Edith, who with her brother looks after her younger brothers and sisters in a derelict apartment. The family live from hand to mouth as they attempt to stay together and avoid being taken into care. Eventually Edith's brother is killed, her youngest sister dies of measles, and the remaining children are placed in an orphanage. The crises in Edith's life help Phyllisia begin to manage her own – to grow up. She stops living in her fantasy world, learns to appreciate her sister, to mourn her mother, to negotiate their powerful and violent father, and to take responsibility for her own actions. At the end of *The Friends*, Phyllisia is only a few months older than she was at the beginning of the book, but she is no longer a child. This is made clear in the closing battle with her father, when she controls the situation, determines the family's future, and understands that emotionally and experientially she is now her father's equal.

One of the most powerful and effective social aspects of realistic writing such as Taylor's and Guy's is that it places the reader in the position of the central character; thus, for a limited period a white middle-class child from the countryside finds him/herself identifying with and seeing the world through the eyes of black children living in Mississippi in the 1930s, Harlem in the 1970s, or, closer to home, a disadvantaged boy from a broken home on a northern council estate (Barry Hines's *Kes*, 1968).

In 1990s Britain, developments in realistic writing for the young are encapsulated in Berlie Doherty's *Dear Nobody* (1991), for which she won the Carnegie Medal. *Dear Nobody* deals with the subjects of teenage pregnancy (still a major social problem), illegitimacy, relationships between the generations, ambition, ambivalence, and love. It is told from two points of view, and draws on established genres such as the epistolary novel and the journal. It begins where it ends: at the moment when the two central characters make the transition from youth to maturity. At first it appears that the rite of passage is the traditional one of leaving home (in this case for university). Chris, the male protagonist, begins the story with a prologue set in his bedroom on the night before he leaves for university. His room has suddenly become 'a door into the past', a space he inhabited when he was 'just a kid'. As the story develops, it becomes clear that the real change in Chris's life has come about not through his leaving home, but with the birth of his daughter. The emotional force of this story (which in itself is, of course, not new) comes from a variety of sources. First, unlike the examples discussed above, the central characters, Chris and Helen, are not typical victims. They belong to caring middle-class families, are well educated, socially sophisticated and ambitious, and, once they discover that Helen is pregnant, they have a number of options open to them. For instance, Helen's parents want her to carry on with her education, and encourage her to have an abortion. Helen is admitted to a clinic and is about to undergo the operation when she realizes that this isn't the right decision for her, and makes up her mind to go through with the pregnancy. At this point familiar forces come into play: the as yet unborn child takes on the old romantic role and brings together the generations by exposing and so exorcising family skeletons. The baby is christened 'Amy', which Chris explains means 'loved one, or friend', and she symbolizes the book's hope that changed social attitudes will make Helen, Chris, and Amy's lives more satisfying than those of their parents and grandparents.

Just as it was necessary to understand the children's literature of the 1890s by looking at the relationship between the social reality and literary construction of childhood, so it is necessary to understand the juvenile fiction of the twentieth-century *fin de siècle* in its social context. In *Dear Nobody* Berlie Doherty encapsulates many of the major changes in the way we understand and define childhood – and indeed the family – which have evolved over the last century. For instance, it is now largely taken for granted that the children of the family (boys *and* girls) will stay at home and in full-time education well into their teens, and that while they are at home they will have their own space, will make several major purchases (among them such things as a music system, television, telephone, computer, fashionable clothes, and possibly a car). As marketing and advertising specialists know, long before they make independent purchases children exercise considerable influence over family expenditure, from choosing what brands to buy in the supermarket to demanding designer clothing, top-name electronic goods, holiday destinations, sport and leisure equipment, and so on.

In the past, the end of childhood was formally signalled by such things as financial independence, leaving home, marriage and/or sexual experience. In the 1990s, all of these significant stages have become blurred. Partly as a consequence of high levels of un-employment and changing government policy, more young people stay in higher education for longer periods than ever before; at the same time, more adults are returning to complete their educations. For similar reasons, young people may delay moving away from home, and prolong their period of financial dependence far beyond the time when most people would regard them as children. Physical maturity and sexual experience both come earlier now than they did 100 years ago,[5] and their consequences are very different. Effective and widely available birth control has changed young people's attitude to and oppor-tunities for sexual activity though, as Aidan Chambers portrays in *The Toll Bridge* (1992), in which two of the central characters succumb to a night of total sexual abandonment, the spread of AIDS (the virus is now in its second decade in Europe) has introduced a new set of problems, fears, and precautions. Chambers deals with this situation, as with so many other important crises that modern young people have to face, in-telligently, openly, and sympathetically. Here the female character, Tess, tells her friend Jan (a boy who secretly watched her and their friend Adam having sex – another taboo confronted) about her anxiety, and it is clear that fear of AIDS has superseded fear of pregnancy:

> Tess sniffed, wiped her nose on the back of her hand. 'Hardly slept since Wednesday.[. . .]And I'll have to see the doctor,' she mumbled.
> Jan tried to take a step back to look her in the face, but she prevented him.
> 'What's the matter? Are you ill?'
> 'He'll give me a heavy lecture, I expect. You'll laugh.'
> 'Why? What about?'
> 'Taking stupid risks, not being responsible.'
> 'What sort of risks?'
> 'Wasn't going to tell you, but . . . Thursday night.[. . .]'
> Jan said, 'I know.'
> 'He told you?'

'No.'

'Guessed?'

'Saw.'[. . .]

Tess squinted at him, tears staunched by an astringent douche of embarrassment.[. . .] 'I will, though, have to see the doc I mean, and I'm worried sick.'

'You'll be OK.'

'How can you say that! How can you know! I was stupid. I've always told myself I'd never be that stupid, but I was, and now I'll have to have awful embarrassing tests and wait until the results come through, and even then, if I'm HIV, nobody can tell for months longer – years – !' She was crying now.

'Hey, hey! Steady!'

'It's all right for you to say that!' (p. 170)

Chambers is one of the most interesting and innovative of our *fin de siècle* writers – both at the level of content and stylistically. In novels such as *Dance on My Grave* (1982) and the earlier *Breaktime* (1978, recently reissued) he deals explicitly, convincingly, and unashamedly with traditionally taboo subjects such as homosexuality and sexual experimentation for both sexes as something which is often (and, he implies, legitimately) done without all the trappings of romantic love. Chambers's characters are frequently witty and sometimes wise, but they are not heroic or exceptional – not idealized links to the past saving the world for future generations – and the dilemmas they face belong very much to the teenage world of the 1990s. What *is* heroic in his texts is not just the decision to deal with the kinds of topics that adults want to keep separate from childhood, but also to employ narrative techniques that disturb or challenge adult notions of what is appropriate for young readers. The whole gamut of modernist and postmodernist experimentation is evoked in his novels. They are self-reflexive and dialogic (that is, employing a variety of different voices), making use of interior monologue, shifting points of view, puns about language, and intertextuality. Chambers always makes the reader think about how language is being employed to tell a story; sometimes he does this by disrupting the story-telling process using tactics such as changing style (say, from realist novel to minimalist playscript), shifting person, or refusing to provide all the usual cohesive ties. At other times he shows the inadequacy of language – and especially

Some of the graphic elements which disrupt the reader's
expectations in *Breaktime*.

The sittingstanding talking man sat.

Fryingpan exploding lightbulbs waterfalled again.

'That was a load of elephant's,' yelled Jack through the cascade.

'All balloon,' said grin-grimacing Ditto.

Robby was Vesuvius before Pompeii got its historic come-uppance.

The hall silence. The standingsittingman stood again.

'stimulating honest peoplecomrade grateful socialist questions'

The again standing standingsittingman sat again.

Robby suddenly was standing at Ditto's sittingside, leaning forward, hands white-knuckled grasping the green tubular steel frame of the infront canvas-covered chair.

'I would like to ask our speaker when, if ever, he intends to demonstrate his solidarity with the working class by putting his considerable income where his not inconsiderable mouth is?'

'Furthermore, does our speaker condemn absolutely the hypocrisy of those who live by preaching the doctrine of socialist change, let's not use the dirty word revolution,'

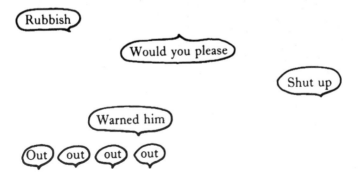

literary language – to convey what it feels like to be in the world. Subjective experience is not unified, orderly, chronological, coherent, and articulate, and life is not a succession of neat episodes. Pages of text (unlike, say, cinematic or televisual images) are peculiarly prone to making stories function in this way, and Chambers works to break up even this physical and habitual aspect of the reading process. An example of his method is *Breaktime*, a novel which sets out systematically to dismantle the young reader's carefully taught expectations of what a novel is. For instance, it constantly calls attention to its own fictionality. One way it does this is by purporting to be written by the central, focalizing character, Ditto, in response to a challenge by his friend, Morgan. Morgan has decided that literature is pointless, and sets out a series of charges against it which conclude:

4. Literature is a GAME, played for FUN, in which the reader *pretends* that he is playing at life. But it is not life. It is a pretence. When you are reading a story you are pretending a lie.
   THEREFORE:
5. Literature is a sham, no longer useful, effluent, CRAP.

Ditto recognizes that the pretence Morgan dislikes derives from his primary objection – its dependence on conventions and its premeditated intentions. Accordingly, he sets out to defend literature by recording what happens to him on a short trip (during which he hopes both to escape temporarily from the problems he has relating to his sick father, and to lose his virginity). His plan is to avoid all the features which make Morgan claim that literature is irrelevant in the modern world. In particular, he intends to disrupt the combined unities of style and plot.

The consequences of this decision are many. For instance, the book can rightly be compared to James Joyce's *Ulysses* as it moves through a vast range of styles, genres, and techniques. Among these are typed essays, graffiti, manifestos, dramatic dialogue, lists, computer graphics, internal monologue, and cartoon speech bubbles. Probably the most radical challenge to the linearity associated with reading comes when Ditto achieves one of his objectives and has sex for the first time. As the experience is transformed into text, the page splits vertically in two. The left-hand column is itself divided into two 'voices'. The first belongs to Ditto-the-narrator. This is signalled by the typeface as well as a recognizably Ditto mode of story telling. In this 'conscious' prose, Ditto seems to be trying to use objective language, relating factually what took place. His attempt is, however, subverted in a number of ways (how deliberate this is supposed to be on Ditto's part is not clear). For instance, the whole tenor of the account is coloured by the discourses of romance and pornography, the conventions which are customarily employed for writing about this subject. Moreover, each line of conscious narration is followed by an italicized line of internal monologue which reveals *one* aspect of the way Ditto is thinking and feeling about what is happening. In this way the text acknowledges that the sexual act doesn't (as the romantic mythology implies) involve total loss of self in the beloved. Thus, at the same time that Ditto is using this – the only language he knows to say what it is he's feeling – it is clear that he is at one level a detached observer, monitoring his experience.

In fact, much of the early portion of the text is primarily concerned with control, as Ditto fights first to *stop* thinking in this detached way – to lose control – and then to control his desire through mental exercises (he recites the nine times tables). As he becomes increasingly excited, his thoughts become more random and characterized by free association ('not done not done not in the oven'). The text finally mimics the moment of orgasm as monosyllabic waves of repeated words engulf what remains of the monologue, which finally ceases.

The effects of this split are powerful. It shows Ditto as simultaneously both observer and subject; the passage overtly combines internal and external positions for narrator and reader. In particular, it successfully illustrates the paradox which results from the primacy and yet the inadequacy of language to convey thought. In order to understand the division of the passage, it is useful to bring to bear on it some of the ideas of the French analyst and critic, Jacques Lacan (1901–81).

The column on the left belongs unequivocally to what Lacan has called the Symbolic Order. For Lacan, the Symbolic Order is represented by the language (both spoken and written) we use to communicate with others and which makes us participating subjects in the social world. Language is undeniably symbolic in that words are obviously not the things they stand for but merely represent them, but for Lacan the Symbolic Order is symbolizing

the air   ha   o god don't laugh
wanted.
laugh   please don't laugh   it's
   But then rising in me, a
not done   not done   not in the oven
gathering of every lusting sensation
yet   ha   o please don't laugh
flowing from every cell of my body
under my spread arm spread hands I feel
to that straining centre, wanted
grass knife-blade-sharp, coarse
body on body, a clutch of source
soil beneath grasp the crystal
of pleasure to whole possession.
earth no grasp her grasp shut it
   I grasped at her. For a fearful
enjoy enjoy enjoy enjoy enjoy enjoy
moment she was gone. But then
shut it words are like boulders
was back again.
thoughts are like broadsides fired
And naked.
against my bodypleasure   why?
As I was
o why?   o sylvan wyeswale
And as eager
is this what makes body
As blind
is this the howdyado   the I'm all
As grasping
right jack   the deflowering of ditto
As clinging
the cider rosie had

months and years
of variation tends
to settle on patterns
which give the
greatest mutual
pleasure. A few
couples even progress
all the way to the
climax of orgasm
while engaged in
the forms of lovemaking
which most people
consider only preliminary—
because in this manner
they reach ecstasy
more surely or
more pleasurably
than by genital
intercourse. For most
couples, however, the
ultimate desire is
for intercourse, in
which the man
inserts his erect
penis into the
woman's vagina. Her
labia and vagina have
been made more moist
than usual by her
excitement, so
the penis can slip in
more easily. The man
has the instinct to

An extract from the orgasm sequence in *Breaktime*.

As sinuous of body
is this the stars in
As flooded with strength
my eyes   my eyes   close my eyes
And energy
in excelsis
And fire.
shut it
She pulled at me,
is this the way
turning me over upon her, urgently,
aboard the lugger
as she fell back upon
and now let
the ground.
battle commence
And gave me entrance
just shut it
with a deep delighting sigh.
shut it
And then there were
shut it
no more
shut
words
it
no more
it
thoughts
It

Nothing but movement

thrust his hips
rhythmically back-
wards and forwards
to move the penis
partly out and in
again, to increase
the sensation for
both. Intercourse
can last fifteen seconds
or a man can learn
to hold back his
orgasm so that
intercourse lasts
for fifteen minutes or
more. As the couple
come nearer to orgasm,
both partners usually
want the rhythmic motion to
become more vigorous
and the woman
may participate in it too.
At the moment of
orgasm—and
generous, experienced
lovers try to make their
climaxes come simultan-
eously—they are
overwhelmed by
five or ten seconds of
intense, pulsating
pleasure
while the ejaculation
occurs, and they cling

something more. Pre-eminently, it represents the division between the conscious which can be articulated) and unconscious (unspeakable) selves. One of Lacan's most famous analogies is that which compares the infant to an 'hommelette' – a mixed-up mass of feelings, desires, and unformed thoughts. Language imposes order on these thoughts by giving the speaker the vocabulary and structure for thinking about and communicating experience, but because both vocabulary and grammar pre-exist the speaker, language can only enable us to say what has already been said or thought. As well, because language supplies 'subject positions' for thinking about the self (I, me, my, mine, he, she, it, and so on) it places the speaker in pre-defined roles, none of which is capable of expressing all the feelings and thoughts that we feel at any given moment. Thus, for Lacan, there is a tension between the Symbolic Order, and what he calls the Imaginary Order: the domain of the unconscious, which is essentially instinctual, inchoate and incommunicable. Just as the unconscious is always trying to make its presence felt by breaking through or otherwise subverting the conscious (through such things as dreams, fantasies, and slips of the tongue), so the Imaginary makes demands on the Symbolic. Essentially, the tension between these two realms (and specifically the fragmented and unstable nature of language) is what Chambers is illustrating in the orgasm sequence in *Breaktime*, where the two orders appear to converge on the page.

Chambers isn't finished here, however, for alongside this battle between the Imaginary and Symbolic orders within the focalizing character runs the text of the right-hand column. This is an extract from *A Young Person's Guide to Life and Love*, by Dr Benjamin Spock, and it provides a running commentary on what is taking place in Ditto's tent from an entirely different perspective. One of the most subtle and effective aspects of the relationship between the two columns is the irony derived from the synchronization of pace and content between Spock's pre-existing discourse on adolescent sexuality and Ditto's attempts at 'live' coverage. For instance, Spock begins with the tautology, 'There's not much point in trying to describe lovemaking', which is, of course, precisely what both he and Ditto are trying to do. As Ditto's language becomes more clichéd, Spock discusses the sources of learned, stereotypical images and vocabularies for talking about sex –

books, movies, and TV. Spock talks about erogenous zones and Helen touches them; Spock describes the technicalities of sexual penetration at the same moment on the page when Ditto enters Helen, and so on. Indeed, Spock's description, intended as a matter-of-fact discussion, is made to function in the manner of a voice-over, and in the process becomes both voyeuristic and remarkably explicit.

The relationship between the two columns is not immediately apparent; indeed, the reader is left to his/her devices to determine whether Spock's is a guide which Ditto has read and internalized (in which case the commentary represents his expectations of what is and will be happening), or whether it is placed on the page to represent an adult, Olympian (e.g. somewhat patronizing, distanced, and detached) view of what is taking place, possibly included for the amusement of Morgan. Its effect is, in any case, to make the reader *think* about the range of discourses available for writing and thinking about sex. Inevitably engaging with the processes of language makes the reader aware of its conventions and our habitualized responses to it.

A final aspect of the right-hand column is that it forces the reader to read the same page of the book for a third time, a process which very effectively breaks the seemingly relentless physical linearity of the book.

Each of the devices described above (and there are many more in *Breaktime*), calls attention to the fact that what we are doing is *reading*, and so the text itself is constantly undermining Morgan's charge that literary conventions insist that the world of the book is real, and that readers are accordingly encouraged to forget that they are reading. The book plays with this idea to the very end, when Morgan reads Ditto's piece and declares it invalid because it is an account of real events, not fiction:

'Of course it isn't [fiction]' bayed Morgan, triumphant. 'We've already agreed about that. It is a record of what happened to you last week.'

'That's what *you* said. I only asked if it convinced you in that respect. You said yes.[. . .]How do you know I didn't sit in my room at home all week making that stuff up?'

[. . .]Morgan made for the door.

'I'm in the thing,' he said as he went. 'Are you saying I'm just a character in a story?'

'Aren't we all?' said Ditto and laughed. (pp. 138-9)

The young reader who has successfully negotiated a novel such as *Breaktime* (and there are others – think of Alan Garner's ground-breaking novels like *The Owl Service*, 1967, *Red-Shift*, 1973, and *The Stone Book* quartet, 1976–8) must find the transition to notoriously 'difficult' writers such as James Joyce, Thomas Pynchon, Jorge Luis Borges and Italo Calvino facilitated. The shift in the kinds of demands being made on readers – of their understanding of narrative technique and ability to play with form – is not confined to teenage fiction. No longer is it assumed that readers have to serve a form of apprenticeship through reading traditional stories and stories told according to the dictates of what has come to be called the 'classic realist text'.[6] Recent years have seen a revolution in the conceptualization of picture books, culminating in the 1990s in the work of Allan and Janet Ahlberg, Anthony Browne, and the team of Jon Scieszka and Lane Smith.

INTERTEXTUALITY AND CHILDREN'S LITERATURE

Our *fin de siècle* picture books make particularly fine use of intertextuality and the related concept of metafiction.[7] Sometimes the demands are primarily visual (for instance, Anthony Browne's allusions to Magritte); sometimes the nature of narrative is explored through conflict between visual and verbal texts (John Burningham is a master of this – see *Come Away from the Water, Shirley*, 1977, and *Time to Get Out of the Bath, Shirley*, 1977). For me, the most exciting examples of picture books are those which hark back to the use of intertextuality discussed earlier in relation to the work of Mrs Sherwood: the texts assume the readers' knowledge of other texts and so, through quotation, references, and other forms of allusion make an alliance between writer and reader, encouraging readers to make connections, bring their knowledge of other texts to bear on the current one, and so simultaneously both to deconstruct and reconstruct it with additional layers.

This kind of playful text reaches its apotheosis in Jon Scieszka and Lane Smith's *The Stinky Cheese Man* (1992). This work draws on even the young child's understanding of 'book', and in something which hovers between the iconoclastic dismantling of the concept and a celebration of it, runs through a non-stop series of jokes and inversions which thoroughly subvert our often unthinking and po-faced acceptance of basic conventions. Nothing in this piece is left unchallenged: type sizes and faces run riot across the pages, the table of contents is found at the end of the first story – indeed it is part of the tale of 'Chicken Licken', for it is not the sky which is falling but the table of contents, which significantly falls and squashes all the characters in that story. In *The Stinky Cheese Man*, narrators and characters argue, the familiar fairy tales on which the book is based laugh at themselves – even the ISBN number and the authors' photographs and biographies are given the same treatment (the standard publicity photographs of author and illustrator are replaced by those of George-I-cannot-tell-a-lie-Washington and Abraham Lincoln). Whereas *Breaktime* ends by reiterating the problematic nature of the relationship between real life and its fictional representation, *The Stinky Cheese Man* states categorically that books are only conventions, and just like rules, conventions are made to be broken. Thus the book begins with the whinging demands of the Little Red Hen, who stands shrieking on the end paper where she is confronted by Jack, the narrator (see pages 60-61).

No reader encountering *The Stinky Cheese Man* can fail to think about what it is that makes a book, where our conventions come from, how they work, what demands they make on the reader, and particularly, the way in which texts get their meaning from what readers bring to them. It is quintessentially 'postmodern', and yet it is also a picture book enjoyed by the under 7s (as well as much older readers). A very different use of intertextuality is found in novels such as Gillian Cross's *Wolf* (1990) and Adele Geras's Egerton Hall trilogy (1990).

Wolf is an elaborate retelling of 'Little Red Riding-Hood', which makes use of fairy tales' grounding in archetypes to explore fear of men and sexuality through the re-enactment of the Oedipal drama experienced by Cassy, its pubescent central character. At the same time it attempts to explain the psychology of terrorism: unbeknownst to her, Cassy's absent father is a notorious IRA bomber. The use of intertextuality in this novel is extremely complex and subtle. Not only is there the understood grounding in and overt references to the well-known fairy tale (Cassy wears a red anorak with a hood, and thinks of the men she meets as

"I have found a kernel of wheat," said the Little Red Hen. "Now who will help me plant this wheat? Where is that lazy dog? Where is that lazy cat? Where is that lazy mouse?"

"Wait a minute. Hold everything. You can't tell your story right here. This is the endpaper. The book hasn't even started yet."

"Who are you? Will you help me plant the wheat?"

"I'm Jack. I'm the narrator. And no, I can't help you plant the wheat. I'm a very busy guy trying to put a book together. Now why don't you just disappear for a few pages. I'll call when I need you."

"But who will help me tell my story? Who will help me draw a picture of the wheat? Who will help me spell 'the wheat'?"

"Listen Hen— forget the wheat. Here comes the Title Page!"

The first two pages of The *Stinky Cheese Man*.

Title Page.

(for The Stinky Cheese Man & Other Fairly Stupid Tales)

PUFFIN BOOKS

wolves), but the tale itself is retold through her dreams. Although the book begins with this epigraph:

> *Of course Cassy never dreams,* Nan always said. *She has more sense, to be sure. Her head touches the pillow and she's off, just like any sensible person. There's been no trouble with dreams, not since she was a baby.* (*Wolf,* p.2)

throughout the text Cassy has not only a recurring nightmare (which the reader quickly recognizes as the story of Little Red Riding-Hood), but one which develops as she begins to understand and confront her fears. As the narrative reaches its climax and Cassy has to rescue her grandmother from the wolf (her son and Cassy's father), the dreams become less fugitive and fragmented, and the feelings they evoke quite clearly mirror the feelings Cassy is experiencing by day. For instance, after a traumatic breakdown during a rehearsal for a performance Cassy is helping prepare for a school workshop, her friend Robert tries to get her to talk about the fears she is repressing behind her stolid, common-sensical manner. 'If things are there,' he tells her, 'you have to admit it in the end.' That night Cassy dreams for the first time about the cottage in the woods (and here, the idea that houses may be metaphors for the self (see page 39) is again useful).

> [. . .]there was the cottage at last, across the clearing. No dark figure was waiting at the gate. No footsteps sounded from the other path. Nothing moved except the woodsmoke rising from the chimney.
>
> And yet –
>
> Did the door always stand ajar? Was there always a line of shadow down the edge? What was inside, hidden in the darkness?
>
> What was inside?
>
> She began to run across the clearing, towards the cottage. Her feet slid on the damp grass. The heavy basket dragged at her arm. Her hand was lifted, ready to knock on the door. Faster and faster and faster she ran.
>
> Without getting any closer[. . .] (*Wolf,* p. 82)

In addition to the intertextual elements provided by the Red Riding-Hood story, *Wolf* also makes use of popular songs ('Who's

Afraid of the Big Bad Wolf'), other fairy tales ('The Three Little Pigs'), werewolf stories, newspaper and magazine articles, encyclopedia entries, medical journals, historical accounts of wolves, television documentary, puns ('I could *wolf* it down'), photographs, and drawings. Each of these sources works on the others to build up a many-faceted image of the cultural meaning of 'wolf', and as the book draws to a close this dialogic representation, in which good and bad are shown not to be mutually exclusive, is brought to bear on the reader's understanding of Cassy's father, Mick Phelan. Mick *is* the Big Bad Wolf – ferocious and unpredictable, prepared to kill even his mother and child for his cause. But Cassy has learned that wolves are more than this – that their public image is largely false. Wolves are also good parents, and never attack needlessly. *Wolf* is certainly not advocating terrorism, and it doesn't play down the cost in human lives, but it does demand that the reader look beneath the propaganda to try to understand the wolf's perspective as well. Equally importantly, it attempts to show that the things which happen to us in childhood don't simply disappear with age – that we are constantly renegotiating our childish selves. Thus, as Cassy has her final dream (which is also her first, long-forgotten, dream), she is already working towards the kind of understanding of the events that have taken place which will make it possible for her to keep the door to her relationship with her father open:

> Cassy lay with her eyes open and gazed into the darkness, making up a letter in her head. *Dear Wolf, Don't vanish into the dark forest again. I still need to know about you. Perhaps I can come and visit you, or . . . or . . .*
>
> Slowly her eyelids drooped. She knew that she wouldn't finish the letter in this dream, but she wasn't worried.
>
> She would write it when she woke up. (p. 140)

Adele Geras also uses the young readers' familiarity with fairy tales to explore topical and often sensitive issues. In *Watching the Roses* (1991), the second of the Egerton Hall stories, she uses the tale of 'Sleeping Beauty' to write about rape and its traumatic after-effects. Her Sleeping Beauty is Alice, who has been raped at her eighteenth birthday party and has withdrawn from the world to deal with her guilt, fear, and sense of violation:

63

Once upon a time, I was a good girl and no trouble to anyone. Now, everyone is worried about me, although I don't think there's really anything that dreadful or strange about me. (p. 7)

Alice longs to be a medieval stone princess; she lies stiff on her bed and refuses to speak. She eats only enough to stay alive, and gradually begins to waste away. Her symptoms are not only those associated with rape victims (especially the sense of guilt – that somehow what has happened is her fault), but also of the anorexic. Alice is rejecting her body and refusing the entry into womanhood that her birthday and the attack, which brings her sexuality unavoidably to the fore, represent. The text is 'written by Alice' in that it purports to be her journal, written at night when everyone else is in bed and she is left to deal with her thoughts. The journal becomes Alice's analyst. She records her dreams, her feelings, her increasing understanding, and her journey towards accepting what has happened and so accepting herself and eventually her Prince Charming (her French pen-friend, Jean-Luc).

Works such as these highlight one aspect of 1990s juvenile fiction: carrying on the work initiated by pioneering writers such as Alan Garner, Penelope Lively and Robert Westall, it has finally broken away from the insistence that children's literature be conservative. That, in the words of Jacqueline Rose, it should contain 'no disturbance at the level of language, no challenge to our [adults'] sexuality, no threat to our status as critics, and no question of our relation to the child.[8] In one way or another, each of the texts discussed above has succeeded in challenging all of these assumptions; however, even in the case of *The Stinky Cheese Man*, the challenges are largely mounted through *words*. Though these texts may no longer portray childhood as safe or innocent, and though they insist on breaking free from the conventions of classic realism, they nonetheless uphold the value of books, and see books as primarily the domain of language. By contrast, a growing range of late-twentieth-century writers has endeavoured to break the linguistic monopoly on fiction, and the result has been the creation of a new genre known as the 'graphic novel'.

COMIC BOOKS AND GRAPHIC NOVELS

Graphic novels use the narrative techniques associated with comic strips – individual frames, speech bubbles, captions, and so on – to tell sustained, and extremely intricate, stories. The reactions of *fin de siècle* parents, educationists, and librarians to graphic fiction has not been unlike that of their nineteenth-century counterparts to what were then called 'penny dreadfuls' and 'bloods' (the popular, highly sensational illustrated magazines which provided tales of pirates, highway men, murderers, and gothic suspense which young people often preferred to the more wholesome and instructive reading their elders wanted them to enjoy). Despite evidence from the past that some of the best writers of their day read these lurid stories avidly, their graphic descendants still stand accused of representing the lowest form of literature – material which is aimed only at those who can aspire to nothing better. Concern continues to be expressed over the levels of violence contained in many examples of graphic fiction, and their impoverished use of language. A particular anxiety at the end of the twentieth century is the attitude to socially vulnerable groups (especially women and ethnic minorities) characteristic of the genre as a whole.

The problematic nature of a large proportion of graphic literature is undeniable, but in recent years it has also generated a number of works of considerable interest and indisputable merit for readers of all ages. For instance, comic-strip elements have been very successfully employed in books for young readers, as can be seen in the distinctive HarperCollins 'Jets'. The virtues of this kind of approach are many; for instance, it makes use of the new readers' pre-existing understanding of visual stories, and specifically their experience of cartoon, commercial, and comic-strip narratives. Another useful quality is that such books, with their mixtures of typefaces and sources of information, are simultaneously more fun and more relevant to the kinds of reading situations they are likely to encounter outside the classroom or the conventional text (for example, posters, magazines, timetables, leaflets). Because of the constant interaction between pictures and text, young readers are able to be presented with vocabulary, ideas, and information which might otherwise appear too difficult (think of the linguistic sophistication of 'Asterix') or disturbing.

Moreover, storytelling in which pictures predominate can be less wordy and daunting to the literary tiro and so encourage greater experimentation (the 'classic comic' retellings of canonical fiction have over the years stimulated many readers' interest in the originals). But graphic literature is not just for the young or inexpert reader. Two examples of graphic novels for older readers (and many would argue that a justification of such works is that they do keep traditionally reluctant groups – especially teenage boys – reading) which demonstrate the potential of this new form are Philip Pullman's *Spring-Heeled Jack* (1989) and Art Spiegelman's *MAUS 1: A Survivor's Tale* (1987).

It would be more accurate to describe *Spring-Heeled Jack* as a hybrid between the conventional and the graphic novel, for each page combines paragraphs of text with comic-strip frames which are integral to the story. It is important to distinguish these frames from illustrations, for they do not simply show what the text has described, but they also advance the plot and contain elements of the written text. For instance, captions will set time, place, atmosphere, and 'cast'; speech bubbles carry much of the dialogue, and illustrations complement or replace description.

Spring-Heeled Jack is set in Victorian London, and its plot is the familiar one of Victorian children escaping from a cruel orphanage to be reunited with a parent who has been presumed dead. The use of this clichéd story-line doesn't result in a derivative story, however, but provides an opportunity to make readers aware of conventions by evoking and then subverting them through humour and pastiche. For instance, the kinds of Victorian novels Pullman is alluding to rely heavily on coincidence to bring about resolution, and *Spring-Heeled Jack* is held together entirely by preposterous coincidences: the children hope to escape to America on the good ship *Indomitable*, which happens to be the same ship on which their despondent father (who has searched fruitlessly for them after returning to England following a mishap at sea) plans to sail to America to start a new life. By coincidence, the sailor who is dispatched to fetch the father's case is engaged to the barmaid to whom Spring-Heeled Jack entrusts the children, and who is eventually put in charge of the orphanage from which they escape . . .

It is not only the conventions of Victorian novels that Pullman

CHAPTER ONE

'It was a dark and stormy night . . .'
Alexandre Dumas, *The Three Musketeers*

It was a dark and stormy night. In the city of London the wind was tossing the boats on the river and driving the rain down every alley, up every flight of steps, and in through every broken window.

No one was out if they had any excuse to stay in. No one respectable, that is. Only alley-cats and criminals had any business in the streets that night, and even they took cover when they could.

High up on the third floor of the Alderman Cawn-Plaster Memorial Orphanage, though, something was stirring.

The first page of *Spring-Heeled Jack* (note the way the text makes playful references to other texts from the outset).

both celebrates and mocks: he also has considerable fun with the semiotic systems of comic strips (helped considerably by the expertise of his illustrator, David Mostyn, of the *Beano*). Thus, on page 79, when the sailor, Jim, announces that he has had a brainwave, his words are followed by a picture of the father's suitcase encased in a 'thought-bubble' which is full of exploding lines to indicate the power of the idea and an arrow linking the word 'brainwave' to the suitcase (which contains the clothes he needs to disguise himself as the children's father and so save them from the orphanage).

With its comic-strip hero (Spring-Heeled Jack is dressed like a Victorian Superman), its use of comic-strip narrative techniques, and its dependence on slapstick humour, *Spring-Heeled Jack* certainly employs many of the elements which have been disparaged by those who deplore graphic fiction. However, Pullman's inclusion of a relatively large proportion of text and the book's covertly conveyed historical content both go some way towards placating (and perhaps wooing) this hostile audience. Texts which make none of these concessions, but which have nevertheless received considerable critical praise, are Art Spiegelman's *MAUS* and its sequel.

MAUS is a graphic approach to the ever-expanding body of literature about the Second World War. It combines biography and autobiography as its narrator Artie, a cartoonist, attempts to tell both the dramatic story of his parents' life in Hitler's Europe and their eventual incarceration in Auschwitz, and the ongoing story of his problematic relationship with his father. *MAUS* is a complex novel, which moves rapidly between past and present, documentary and psycho-drama, personal and cultural history. Spiegelman uses only cartoon techniques to tell his story, and this has several interesting but potentially contentious consequences. For instance, like many cartoonists and satirists, he has decided to substitute animals for human characters, and not just on an individual basis – in *MAUS*, animal species represent racial and national groups. Thus the German Nazis are portrayed as cats, the Jews as mice, the Poles as pigs, and the Americans as dogs. This decision leads to some difficult questions: is the text suggesting that since it is natural for cats to terrorize and kill mice it was in some way 'natural' for the Nazis to persecute and execute the Jews? Portraying the Poles as pigs – animals regarded by

Jews as 'unclean' – is equally ambiguous. Perhaps the most important effect of the cartoon approach is to make it possible to tell afresh what has become a familiar story, and one which, like the horrendous footage from famine-stricken countries and war zones, it is so painful to hear that defensive strategies rapidly desensitize us. There is nothing infantile about MAUS, and it certainly does not deserve to be stigmatized as 'sub-literature' because it makes use of comic-strip story-telling techniques.

SUBVERSION AND JUVENILE FICTION

Though MAUS and a range of other graphic texts may be held up as exemplars, concerns about the attitudes typical of much of the genre are justified. In particular, the high incidence of violence specifically directed against women, homosexuals and members of ethnic minorities is disturbing and distasteful. Without in any way wishing to legitimize these tendencies, it is important to try to understand where they come from. This is a huge task – a sociological investigation far beyond the scope of this study – but there are some issues which relate directly to young people's reading which can be addressed.

As was discussed briefly in relation to 'penny dreadfuls' and 'bloods', there has always been a tension between what children want to read and what adults think they ought to read. In the past, young people's preferences were generally dismissed as 'rubbish' – at best lacking literary merit; at worst positively harmful because of the dubious values, misinformation, and linguistic errors they contained. In the second half of this century, however, the debate has changed. In a short piece for Children's Literature in Education, Peter Dickinson defined 'rubbish' as 'all forms of reading matter which contain to the adult eye no visible value, either aesthetic or educational'.[9] Dickinson went on to argue that such reading matter was not valueless to the child, as it served both psychological needs (allowing the maturing child to relax and regress) and fostered independent judgement through experimentation and comparison. Bruno Bettelheim's study of the meaning and importance of fairy tales argued that the child uses fairy tales (and by extension all imaginative stories) to deal with

Artie tells the story of his life through his father's life-story in
MAUS I: A Survivor's Tale.

conflicts between inner and outer worlds, needs, and demands, and his work was influential in encouraging adults to accept that often children find value in books which seem to have little or no merit to more experienced readers. Indeed, a growing number of critics now argue that the fact that adults find such reading matter repugnant or at least valueless is important to young readers. In *Don't Tell the Grown-Ups* (1990), Alison Lurie suggests one of the great pleasures of children's fiction for its intended audience is its potential to undermine and subvert the adult world. Nowhere is this tendency more apparent than in many of the most popular forms of 'rubbish' (for instance comics, the works of Roald Dahl, and lyrics to popular music), which overtly mock the values and behaviour which often seem to obsess parents, teachers, and adult-run institutions. Foremost among these are the need to be tidy, hard-working, polite, studious, careful about money, uninterested in sex, socially acceptable, and so on. 'Rubbish' of this sort is part of a subculture to which all adults once belonged. It changes very little from generation to generation, and serves as a healthy reminder that part of growing up has traditionally involved forgetting the value systems of childhood. The conflict between adult and childhood values has underpinned both ends of the juvenile canon – from *Peter Pan* (and its contemporary cinematic reworking, Steven Spielberg's *Hook*, 1991) and *The Secret Garden* to the *Dandy* and *Matilda* (1989). The 'Great Tradition' in children's literature has always been characterized by its elevation of childhood and its questioning of adult wisdom and orthodoxy. But a new dynamic has entered the situation. Just as parents at the end of the last century were investing more and more in childhood in response to social changes, so late-twentieth-century parents, the majority of whom grew up in the liberal 1960s, have changed the boundaries of what constitutes 'rubbish'. Greater understanding of young people's needs, the mass-media attention to youth culture, a tendency to admire rebels, and a wide-spread reluctance to 'hang up their rock'n roll shoes' have meant that much which had previously been classified as 'rubbish' is now officially approved and purchased by parents. The consequence is, of course, that new forms of subversion have to be found, and the cults of violence and horror seem to fulfil this function admirably, as demonstrated by the widespread popularity of writers such as Stephen King and copy-cat series for younger readers like the highly successful 'Point Horror' stories published by Scholastic Children's Book Publishers!

With their emphasis on violence, aggression, horror, and the bizarre, series such as these seem to represent both the apotheosis and the nadir of contemporary fantasy for young people. They are symptomatic of what Rosemary Jackson has described as the debilitating psychological effects of inhabitating a materialistic culture stimulated by a capitalist economy: 'peculiarly violent and horrific'.[10] However, as with all social phenomena, simple explanations are inadequate. Considerable research has been done on the consequences of viewing violence, but very little time has been given to the effects of *reading* about violence. One person who has begun to work in this area is Charles Sarland. In *Young People Reading: Culture and Response* (Milton Keynes, 1991) he looks at pupils' responses to reading and viewing violent texts and screened adaptations of them (for instance, Stephen King's *Carrie*). An extremely interesting difference between the way boys and girls read the texts began to emerge; specifically, that girls – often the victim figures in both versions – frequently seemed to be able to read across the text. For example, they found the most posturing and unrelieved machismo of ostensibly the most violent and dangerous characters humorous and unconvincing. Instead of being frightened by the scenarios the books construct, they found in them an opportunity for feeling superior.

While it may be true that texts which sensationalize and/or celebrate violence fulfil some useful functions and for some groups of readers actually seem to deconstruct many of the myths which circulate around aggressive behaviour, the underlying ideology they espouse, with its emphasis on the mastery of 'inferior' social groups by largely white, physically powerful, male authority figures is unlikely to find widespread acceptance and approval amongst those working in children's literature. This is not to say that violence has no place in juvenile fiction. Some of the most powerful contemporary texts deal with extremes of violence: from the violence used to suppress generations of African Americans (Mildred D. Taylor and Paula Fox) to the consequences of the religious and political divisions in Ireland (Joan Lingard), through the savage repressions of Stalinism (Anne Holm), the unimaginable atrocities perpetrated during war (Alick Rowe), the devastation of nuclear holocaust (Robert O'Brien), and, equally devastating, the psychological and physical barbarities inflicted by young people on each other (Robert Cormier). The difference between the violence portrayed in these books and that of the horror genre is that in horror violence is titilating, gratuitous, and not cathartic, so it neither tells the reader something about violence nor releases pent-up emotions. Horror creates and feeds an appetite for violence, while, in the literary explorations of even the bleakest of the writers mentioned above, violence is interrogated and confronted, and ultimately dismissed as misguided and sickening.

CHILDREN'S LITERATURE AND THE NATIONAL CURRICULUM

Young people's reading of violent texts also feeds into another area of anxiety which is directly related to the social meaning of childhood at this *fin de siècle*. This can most readily be seen by looking at the debates which have raged around the teaching of literature within the National Curriculum.

The ideological centrality of children's literature is nowhere more apparent than in the battles which have been waged over the recommended texts and official anthologies prescribed by the National Curriculum Council (the National Curriculum itself is a *fin de siècle* phenomenon which came into force in 1989 and can in many ways be seen to parallel the aspirations and values which underpinned the Education Acts of the closing decades of the last century).

The NCC recommendations and anthologies are largely made up of works which represent the late-Victorian/Edwardian myth of the 'Beautiful Child': no doubt a reaction on the part of many adults to other problems associated with children today. At the time of writing a child of 9 is in the news for causing the death of a pensioner (who had previously been beaten and bullied by a gang of children); a 16-year-old has been arrested for murdering a younger boy in a park while the boy's family watched a game of cricket; earlier this year two children abducted and murdered a toddler, and police across the country have found themselves in the difficult position of not being able to prosecute under-age offenders involved in serious and dangerous activities such as joy riding, burglary, drug dealing, and prostitution. Although changes in legislation mean that children under the age of 10 cannot be held criminally responsible for their actions (until 1908 children were tried and sentenced in exactly the same ways – and sent to the same institutions or places of executions – as adults), for many urban children at the end of the twentieth century, life is in many ways as difficult and frightening as it was in the days of Mayhew's Watercress Girl. At the end of the 1980s, Humphries, Mack, and Perks summed up the situation:

> For children of the poor and unemployed who live in the city slums, childhood often remains short and brutal. Some of the poorest children on city 'sink' estates become 'street wise' at a very early age. Addiction to hard drugs, like heroin, and street crime are now beginning to be recognised as problems among younger and younger children. Being found guilty of mugging is not uncommon among eight and nine year olds in the most deprived parts of large cities.[11]

Given that this is the case for a substantial proportion of British children; that many of those who are financially and domestically secure come from vastly different cultures, and that our understanding of the needs and realities of childhood has moved so far from the fantasies of Lewis Carroll, J. M. Barrie and A. A. Milne, the NCC's attempts to reinstate the values and images of the 'Beautiful Child' (who, it seems, must speak Standard English) seem both misguided and suspect. Writing in *The Times* (1 January 1993), Sally Feldman summed up the position thus:

> The new book lists drawn up by the National Curriculum Council are a betrayal of children, of their literature, and of the experience of reading. Gone are the principles . . . variety, richness of experience, reflecting the multi-cultural nature of today's society. Back in are the classics, defined so rigidly that the list would not, for the most part, have been out of place in the library at Greyfriars.[. . .]So why have our best contemporary writers been ignored in favour of this outmoded spectre of childhood, frozen in a sentimental, ultra-traditional frame? [. . .]The culture offered to our children is dominated by the values of the British empire in its heyday. The books are mostly written from the point of view of the English upper middle classes for their children. [. . .]These lists present[. . .]a swingeing denial of what is good and valuable in modern writing, choosing instead to create a new two-tier system – the ones who can manage *Treasure Island* and *Oliver Twist*, and the failures.

It should be said here that teachers, who perhaps more than any other group see children stripped of the trappings of the 'Beautiful Child', have, with increasing success, resisted and rejected many of the NCC's attempts to create a syllabus which unashamedly wants a return to some mythical notion of 'Victorian values', when women, children, and other cultures bowed before Britain's patriarchs. An important feature of the work undertaken in schools has been a consistent downgrading of the supremacy of 'the canon' (those books, almost invariably written by dead, white, European males – DWEMs – and which for decades were believed to represent the best in literature), and with it an appreciation of alternative forms of writing, including those which are most relevant to pupils from different cultural backgrounds.

While some stimulating texts have resulted from this cross-fertilization of literary cultures, internationalism in juvenile fiction is not invariably a positive force. The ethos behind international organizations such as the International Board on Books for Young People (IBBY) *is* admirable. IBBY was founded after the Second World War in the belief that encouraging children from different nations to read each others' literature would lead to greater understanding between them and so make the possibility of a third world war less likely. The practicalities of publishing and translating books in different languages has limited what such organizations have been able to achieve. However, a new commercial form of internationalism is being extremely successful in financial terms, though its effects have generally been not to improve quality and diversity in children's publishing. Publishers need to produce books which will sell around the world, and this almost invariably means books which are the literary equivalent of airport architecture – when reading them you could be anywhere, or nowhere. Typical examples of this phenomenon are 'The REAL Ghostbuster' and 'Teenage Mutant Ninja Turtle' books and comics, and Colin Dann's *The Animals of Farthing Wood*. The first Farthing Wood book appeared in 1979; by the 1990s there were five sequels and a number of versions of the main story, including an abridged version for younger readers and two picture books. *The Animals of Farthing Wood* itself was reprinted fourteen times between 1990 and 1993, and has over this period been a 'bestseller'. The appeal of this highly derivative animal epic must reside largely in its ability to be inoffensive: using animals makes it easy to avoid problems of race, nationality, and class; thus it was possible to market the book and its many spin-offs in a large number of countries. Since it first appeared in book form *The Animals of Farthing Wood* has been translated into most major languages, been turned into an internationally marketed cartoon, and in 1992 a well co-ordinated advertising campaign launched *The Animals of Farthing Wood* magazine in most European countries simultaneously. Undoubtedly the huge success of this book and its sequels is due to their marketing potential rather than any intrinsic merit.

CONCLUSION

It would be wrong to end this study by concluding that children's literature at the end of the twentieth century is on the way to becoming a bland and bogus international product. The truth is that the range and diversity of contemporary writing for children has never been greater. In every aspect of the juvenile publishing industry – from picture books through fantasy, history, myth, realist novels, adventure, mystery, horror, romance, and so on and so on, innovative, stimulating, and impressive books for readers of all ages and abilities are being produced. The first part of this book ended by looking at the consequences of publishing decisions made at the end of the nineteenth century and which have continued to influence contemporary publishing; specifically with regard to gender. It seems appropriate, then, to end this section by looking at the work of two women writers at the end of this century who have gone a long way towards ridding us of these residual influences: Diana Wynne Jones and Anne Fine.

Diana Wynne Jones is a highly skilled and innovative writer of fantasy. All of her books explore the relationship between fantasy and reality in a particularly pointed way. Fantasy usually involves the creation of an alternative world which is temporarily entered by protagonists (and readers). Diana Wynne Jones certainly creates alternative worlds, but while in most fantasy there is a link or correspondence between what happens in the fantasy world and what happens in the 'real' world of the text (for instance, the child who conquers his/her problems in the fantasy world usually finds that previously troubling situations in the real world have diminished or been resolved), in Jones's stories the relationship between these worlds is rather different. Her books generally assume that what seems to be a fantasy to her readers is reality elsewhere, and that the tendency for most people to relegate what seems to be improbable to the realms of fantasy is a learned response. This gives her an interest in both history and ideology which she works out to great (often comic) effect. For instance, she looks at the paradox that in twentieth-century Britain it is usual to train children to be rationalists while feeding them on a diet of stories which consists largely of anti-rationalist material (fairy tales, stories about witches, talking animals, magic powers – all kinds of 'fantasies'). What if, she asks, the stories are true and the rationalist stance mistaken? After all, at other times and in other cultures people did/do believe in magic, witchcraft, and the supernatural – perhaps our culture has lost this capacity. And if it has lost it, how did this come about?

This way of thinking underpins a number of Diana Wynne Jones's most popular books, and it enables her to hold up the world we know for examination. Her stories show that even what appear to be the most fundamental aspects of society have come about through human actions and decisions (history), and that nothing about the way we organize our lives is inevitable or natural.

One of the ways she often sets about deconstructing the reader's assumptions about the world is to base the story in an alternative world for which twentieth-century British society is a fantasy. This has the dual effect of normalizing what would otherwise be improbable behaviour, and making the familiar world seem strange. For instance, the three linked books *Charmed Life* (1977), *Witch Week* (1985), and *The Lives of Christopher Chant* (1988) all explore what it would be like to live in a world where magic was normal. Each features characters who are in every way like us – except they can do magic (and this is perfectly ordinary). Thus, *The Lives of Christopher Chant* begins:

> It was years before Christopher told anyone about his dreams. This was mostly because he lived in the nurseries at the top of the big London house, and the nursery maids who looked after him changed every few months. (p. 7)

Christopher lives in London, his parents go walking in the park, he has a succession of governesses and goes to boarding school – and he is also magic, as are all the other characters in the book. Christopher's dreams are in fact trances which enable him to travel to a series of parallel worlds which have evolved in different ways. In some there are dragons, in others mermaids, and in one there is no magic at all because people have stopped believing in it . . . This is a dangerous, ugly, and noisy world, and recognizably our own. How magic came to be lost is explained in *Witch Week*, which uses key events in history as the moments which divide parallel worlds. Thus, each time a world gets to a crisis, in this case Guy Fawkes's attempt to blow up Parliament, several possibilities for its development exist. For instance, Guy Fawkes could succeed and escape; succeed and be caught; fail and escape; fail and be caught; be too frightened to go through with it; and so on. Each of these possibilities is then played out in a different parallel world; the world we know is one which at some point decided not to believe in magic and witchcraft.

The significance of this kind of thinking for young readers at the end of the twentieth century is that it raises a range of questions about how the world can and should develop over the next hundred years. The factors which influence and organize our life – from gender, race, and class to science and logic – are not perceived as given and absolute. The reader is left asking, 'what if white Christians were the ethnic minority?'; 'what if women were more powerful than men?' This way of thinking makes it possible to identify and interrogate social practice, and promotes individual, independent thinking.

Diana Wynne Jones's way of promoting social change is subtle and generalized. By contrast, Ann Fine tackles specific issues very directly, as can be seen in the attack she mounts on gender stereotyping in *Bill's New Frock* (1990). The plot is very simple. One morning Bill Simpson wakes up to discover that he's been turned into a girl. Perhaps unintentionally, this beginning is remarkably similar to that of Kafka's *Metamorphosis*, in which the central character wakes up to discover he's been turned into a beetle. The result of this similarity is, rather unfortunately, to suggest that girls are like beetles. But with this exception, Fine's books provides a wonderfully funny and effective way of looking at habitualized responses to children on the basis of their sex.

"Hurry up with the meal, Mum," the boys called every evening when they came home from their very important school.

"Hurry up with the meal, old girl,"
Mr Piggott called every evening when
he came home from his very important job.

A number of contemporary authors and illustrators have dealt with the problem of sexism in children's literature, as can be seen in these pages from Anthony Browne's *Piggybook* (1986). Take a close look at Mr Piggott's shadow and newspaper!

Bill is amazed to discover that now he is a girl he is supposed to work more quietly and neatly; that there are huge areas of the playground forbidden him; that he's expected to lose a race deliberately so that a handicapped child can win; that he's overlooked for active jobs and overburdened with responsible ones, and that he can't even read the comics he wants to at playtime. For the purposes of this discussion, the most important moment of the book comes when Bill's table is chosen to read the morning's story, 'Rapunzel'. Bill finds himself both denied the role of hero/prince and unable to identify with the passive Rapunzel, locked up in her tower and submissively lowering her locks to order:

> No, it wasn't much of a part. Or much of a life, come to that, if you thought about it.
>
> Bill raised his hand. He couldn't help it.[. . .]'I don't see why Rapunzel just has to sit and wait for the Prince to come along and rescue her,' explained Bill. 'Why couldn't she plan her own escape? Why didn't she cut off all her lovely long hair herself, and braid it into a rope, and knot the rope to something, and then slide down it? Why did she have to just sit there and waste fifteen years waiting for a prince?'
>
> Mrs Collins narrowed her eyes at Bill Simpson.
>
> 'You're in a funny mood today,' she told him. 'Are you sure you're feeling yourself?' (pp. 21-2)

By the middle of a single day as a girl, and despite the fact that he still thinks of himself as a boy (terribly confusing in the loo!), Bill has been rendered inarticulate and has resigned himself to accepting passively whatever happens to him. When the teacher takes his hand and gets him to sit so that his classmates can paint pictures of him in his pretty pink frock, he

> could have tried to say something[. . .]but he didn't bother. He reckoned there was no point.[. . .]A curse was on him. A pink curse. He was, of all things, haunted by a pretty pink frock with fiddly shell buttons. He might as well give up struggling. Like poor Rapunzel trapped in her high stone tower, he'd just sit quietly, waiting to see what happened, hoping for rescue. (p. 40)

While clearly accelerated and exaggerated for the purposes of getting young readers to think about why life is so different for

Bill simply because people think he's a girl, Fine's book nevertheless relies on well-documented differences in expectation and handling of children of different sex at school (see McRobbie, 1984 and Walkerdine, 1984[12]). Bill's frustration and eventual resignation at his treatment and inability to alter it are made more vivid and potent because they are new to him and not what he expects after even a short lifetime's experience of consciously and unconsciously sexist encounters from the male point of view.

Fine's work is not unique. Sensitivity to the problems associated with sex-role stereotyping is reflected in the work of many late-twentieth-century writers and illustrators, including those responsible for school reading schemes. However, what *Bill's New Frock* succeeds in doing very well is highlighting the anachronistic conventions originating in the nineteenth-century *fin de siècle* yet still present in much contemporary juvenile fiction. *Bill's New Frock* reminds us that the relationship between children's reading and the reproduction of social attitudes and behaviour – like those which underpin residual ideas about gender – needs to be better understood and more fully explored by writers, publishers, purchasers, and, most important of all, young readers themselves.

Notes

CHAPTER 1. FOREVER YOUNG: FANTASIES OF CHILDHOOD

1 See P. Ariès, *Centuries of Childhood*, trans. R. Baldick (London, 1962); L. Stone, *The Family, Sex and Marriage in England 1500-1800* (London, 1977); L. Pollock, *Forgotten Children: Parent – Child Relationships from 1500 to 1900* (Cambridge, 1983); K. Thomas, 'Children in Early Modern England', in *Children and Their Books: A Celebration of the Work of Iona and Peter Opie*, ed. G. Avery and J. Briggs (Oxford, 1989); C. J. Sommerville, *The Discovery of Childhood in Puritan England* (London, 1992).

2 Leonore Davidoff, 'Class and Gender in Victorian England', in *Sex and Class in Women's History*, ed. J. Newton, M. Ryan and J. Walkwitz (London, 1983).

3 Quoted in W. E. Houghton, *The Victorian Frame of Mind, 1830–1870* (London, 1957), p. 355.

4 F. Cott, 'Passionlessness: An Interpretation of Victorian Sexual Ideology, 1790-1850', in *Signs*, 4, 2 (1978), pp. 219-36; K. Reynolds and N. Humble, *Victorian Heroines: Readings and Representations of Femininity in Nineteenth-Century Literature and Art* (Hemel Hempstead, 1993).

5 See E. Showalter, *Sexual Anarchy: Gender and culture at the fin de siècle* (London, 1992).

6 See R. Benedict, 'Continuities and discontinuities in cultural conditioning', *Psychiatry*, 1; M. Mitterauer, *A History of Youth*, trans. G. Dunphy (Oxford, 1986).

7 R. Barthes, *Mythologies*, trans. A. Lavers (1957; London, 1972).

8 J. Stephens, *Language and Ideology in Children's Fiction* (Harlow, 1992), p. ix.

9 See K. Reynolds, *Girls Only? Gender and Popular Children's Fiction in Britain 1880-1910* (Hemel Hempstead, 1990).

10 H. Carpenter, *Secret Gardens: A Study of the Golden Age of Children's Literature* (London 1985).

11 G. Rattray Taylor, *The Angel Makers: A Study in the Psychological*

Origins of Historical Change, 1750-1850 (London, 1973); C. J. Sommerville, *The Discovery of Childhood in Puritan England.*

12 M. Tatar, *Off With Their Heads! Fairy tales and the culture of childhood* (London, 1992), epigraph.

13 See Stephens, *Language and Ideology in Children's Fiction.*

14 Z. Shavit, *The Poetics of Children's Literature* (Athens, Ga., 1986).

15 M. Foucault, *The Order of Things: An Archaeology of the Human Sciences* (1966; trans. London, 1970), p. 50.

16 S. Humphries, J. Mack and R. Perks, *A Century of Childhood* (London, 1988), pp. 39-40.

17 See L. Stone, *The Family, Sex and Marriage in England 1500–1800* (London, 1977); J. M. Goldstrom, *Education: Elementary Education 1780–1900* (Newton Abbot, 1972); J. Purvis, 'The Experience of Schooling for Working-Class Boys and Girls in Nineteenth-Century England', in *Defining the Curriculum: Histories and Ethnographies'*, ed. I. Goodson and S. Ball (Barcombe, 1984); K. Reynolds, *Girls Only? Gender and Popular Children's Fiction in Britain 1880-1910.*

18 H. Mayhew, *London Labour and the London Poor* (New York, 1968), vol. 1, pp. 45-8.

19 H. Michie, *The Flesh Made Word: Female Figures and Women's Bodies* (Oxford, 1987).

20 P. Brooks, 'Towards Supreme Fictions', in *Yale French Studies: The Child's Part*, ed. P. Brooks (New Haven, Conn., 1969), p. 9.

21 See F. Hughes, in *Children's Literature: The development of criticism*, ed. P. Hunt (London, 1990).

22 In G. Avery and J. Briggs (eds), *Children and Their Books: A Celebration of the Work of Iona and Peter Opie* (Oxford, 1989).

23 Avery and Briggs, *Children and Their Books*, p. 248.

CHAPTER 2. GROWING UP IS HARD TO DO

1 J. Dollimore, in A. Sinfield, *Society and Literature 1945–1970* (London, 1983), p. 61.

2 See L. Rosenthal, 'The Development of Consciousness in Lucy Boston's *The Children of Green Knowe*', in *The Modern Language Association's Children's Literature Association Journal* (Newhaven, Conn. and London, 1980).

3 See N. Chodorow, *The Reproduction of Mothering: Psychoanalysis and the Sociology of Gender* (Berkeley and Los Angeles, 1978).

4 See A. Sinfield, *Society and Literature 1945–1970.*

5 M. Mitterauer, *A History of Youth*, trans. G. Dunphy (1986; Oxford, 1992), p. 3.

6 See C. Belsey, *Critical Practice* (London, 1980), ch. 3.

7 See G. Moss, in *Literature for Children: Contemporary Criticism*, ed. P. Hunt (London, 1992).

8 J. Rose, *The Case of 'Peter Pan', or The Impossibility of Children's Fiction* (London, 1984), p. 20.

9 In *Children's Literature in Education* (London, 1970), repr. in G. Fox *et al.* (eds) , *Writers, Critics and Children* (London, 1976) p. 74.

10 In C. Sarland, *Young People Reading: Culture and Response* (Milton Keynes, 1991), p. 63.

11 S. Humphries, J. Mack and R. Perks, *A Century of Childhood*, (London, 1988) p. 35.

12 A. McRobbie and M. Nava, *Gender and Generation*, (London, 1984); V. Walkerdine, 'On the Regulation of Speaking and Silence: Subjectivity, Class and Gender in Comtemporary Schooling', in *Language, Gender and Childhood*, ed. C. Steedman, C. Urwin, and V. Walkerdine (London, 1984).

Select Bibliography

The following list contains all the sources used in the process of preparing this study. Whereas references in the text give the date of first publication, references in this list are to the editions with which I have worked. I have added comments on those texts which are particularly useful as general references on the various subjects covered – children's literature, childhood, and critical studies of children's literature.

In addition to scholarly studies, it is often useful (and enjoyable) to read individual accounts of growing up in particular periods. For instance, Flora Thompson's well-known autobiography, *Lark Rise to Candleford* (available in a Penguin paperback edition) gives a vivid description of the life of a rural child in the second half of the nineteenth century. Biographies and autobiographies of many of the writers discussed in this study are also widely available.

WORKS OF FICTION

The following works are mentioned in the text. They by no means constitute an exhaustive list; such a task would more than fill a book in itself since in the 1990s alone the UK has regularly produced in excess of 5,000 children's books annually.

Nineteenth century

Anstey, Frederick, *Vice-Versa, or, A Lesson to Fathers* (London: Smith and Elder, 1882).
Barrie, J. M., *The Little White Bird* (London: Hodder and Stoughton, 1902).
—*Peter Pan* (Harmondsworth: Puffin, 1970).
Burnett, Frances Hodgson, *Little Lord Fauntleroy* (London: Frederick Warne, 1886).

—*The Secret Garden* (Harmondsworth: Puffin, 1951).

Edgeworth, Maria, *The Parents' Assistant* (London: 1796).

Farrar, Frederick, *Eric, or Little by Little* (London: S. W. Partridge and Co., undated).

Fielding, Sarah, *The Governess or The Little Female Academy* (London: Oxford University Press, 1968).

Grahame, Kenneth, *Dream Days* (London: Thomas Nelson, undated).

—*The Golden Age* (London: Thomas Nelson, 1895).

—*The Wind in the Willows* (London: Scribners, 1954).

Hoffmann, Heinrich, *The English Struwwelpeter, or Pretty Stories and Funny Pictures for Little Children* (Leipzig: Friedrich Volckmar, 1848).

James, Henry, *What Maisie Knew* (Harmondsworth: Penguin, 1988).

Kipling, Rudyard, *Stalky & Co.* (London: Macmillan, 1908).

Lang, Andrew, *The Blue Fairy Book* (London: Longman and Green, 1899).

—*The Lilac Fairy Book* (New York: Dover, 1982).

—*Prince Prigio* (London: J. M. Dent, 1961).

—*Prince Ricardo of Pantouflia* (London: J. M. Dent, 1961).

Meade, L. T. *A Sweet Girl Graduate* (London: Cassell & Co., 1897).

Rousseau, Jean Jacques, *Emile*, trans. Barbara Foxley (London: J. M. Dent, 1911).

Sherwood, Mary Martha, *The Fairchild Family* (London: Hatchard, 1818).

Stretton, Hesba, *Jessica's First Prayer* (London: Religious Tract Society, undated).

—*Little Meg's Children* (London: Religious Tract Society, undated).

Wilde, Oscar, *The Happy Prince* and *The Selfish Giant*, in *Complete Works of Oscar Wilde*, intro. Vyvyan Holland (London: Collins, 1969).

—*A House of Pomegranates* (London: Garland, 1977).

—*The Picture of Dorian Gray* (New York: Signet, 1962).

Twentieth century

Boston, Lucy, M., *The Children of Green Knowe* (Harmondsworth: Puffin, 1987).

Browne, Anthony, *Piggybook* (London: Mammoth, 1991).

Burningham, John, *Come Away from the Water, Shirley* (London: Cape, 1977).

—*Time to get out of the Bath, Shirley* (London: Cape, 1978).

Chambers, Aidan, *Breaktime* (London: Bodley Head, 1978).

—*Dance on my Grave* (London: Bodley Head, 1982).

—*The Toll Bridge* (London: Bodley Head, 1992).

Cross, Gillian, *Wolf* (Harmondsworth: Puffin, 1992).

Dahl, Roald, *Matilda* (Harmondsworth: Puffin, 1989).

Dann, Colin, *The Animals of Farthing Wood* (London: Mammoth, 1993).

Doherty, Berlie, *Dear Nobody* (London: HarperCollins, 1992).

Fine, Anne, *Bill's New Frock* (London: Mammoth, 1990).

Garner, Alan, *The Owl Service* (London: Collins, 1984).

—*Red-Shift* (London: Collins, 1973).

—*The Stone Book Quartet* (London: Collins, 1983).

Geras, Adele, *Watching the Roses* (London: HarperCollins, 1991).

Guy, Rosa, *The Friends* (Harmondsworth: Puffin, 1987).

Jones, Diana Wynne, *Charmed Life* (Harmondsworth: Puffin, 1980).

—*The Lives of Christopher Chant* (London: Mammoth, 1989).

—*Witch Week* (London: Mammoth, 1990).

Laird, Elizabeth, *Kiss the Dust* (London: Mammoth, 1991).

Milne, A. A., *The House at Pooh Corner* (London: Methuen, 1960).

—*Winnie the Pooh* (London: Methuen, 1966).

Norton, Mary, *The Borrowers* (London: J. M. Dent, 1968).

Pearce, Philippa, *Tom's Midnight Garden* (Harmondsworth: Puffin, 1976).

Pullman, Philip, *Spring-Heeled Jack* (London: Yearling, 1991).

Scieszka, John, and Smith, Lane, *The Stinky Cheese Man* (Harmondsworth: Puffin, 1993).

Spiegelman, Art, *MAUS 1: A Survivor's Tale* (Harmondsworth: Viking/Penguin, 1987).

Storr, Catherine, *Marianne Dreams* (Harmondsworth: Puffin, 1968).

Taylor, Mildred D., *Roll of Thunder, Hear My Cry* (Harmondsworth: Penguin, 1988).

Westall, Robert, *Gulf* (London: Methuen, 1992).

CRITICAL AND HISTORICAL STUDIES

Althusser, A., trans. as 'Ideology and Ideological State Apparatuses', in *Lenin and Philosophy and Other Essays* (London: New Left Books, 1977).

Ariès, Philippe, *Centuries of Childhood*, trans. R. Baldrick (London: Jonathan Cape, 1962). One of the most influential studies of childhood ever written. Largely on the basis of pictorial representations of childhood, Ariès argues that the concept of childhood is relatively modern. For a variety of reasons, among them high birth rates and almost equally high rates of infant mortality, Ariès concludes childhood was not a phase which was valued or understood. In short, he says childhood 'did not exist'.

Avery, G., *Nineteenth-Century Children: Heroes and heroines in English children's stories 1780-1900* (London: Hodder and Stoughton, 1965).

Avery, Gillian, and Julia Briggs (eds), *Children and Their Books: A Celebration of the Work of Iona and Peter Opie* (Oxford: Clarendon Press,

1989). A wide-ranging collection of stimulating essays on the history of children's book publishing, childhood, well-known authors, illustrators, and issues in children's literature.

Barthes, R., *Mythologies*, trans. A. Lavers (1957; London: Paladin, 1972).

Belsey, C., *Critical Practice* (London: Methuen, 1980).

Benedict, R., 'Continuities and discontinuities in cultural conditioning', *Psychiatry*, 1 (1938).

Benevenuto, B., and R. Kennedy, *The Works of Jacques Lacan: An Introduction* (London: Free Association Books, 1986).

Bettelheim, B., *The Uses of Enchantment: The Meaning and Importance of Fairy Tales* (London: Thames and Hudson, 1976).

Bratton, J. S., *The Impact of Victorian Children's Fiction* (London: Croom Helm, 1981).

Briggs, J., 'Women Writers and Writing for Children: From Sarah Fielding to E. Nesbit', in G. Avery and J. Briggs (eds), *Children and Their Books: A Celebration of the Work of Iona and Peter Opie* (Oxford: Clarendon Press, 1989).

Bristow, J., *Empire Boys: Adventures in a Man's World* (London: Harper-Collins, 1991).

Brooks, P., 'Towards Supreme Fictions', in P. Brooks (ed.) *Yale French Studies: The Child's Part* (New Haven: Yale University Press, 1969).

Cadogan, M., and P. Craig, *You're a Brick, Angela! The girls' story 1839–1985* (London: Victor Gollancz, 1986).

Carpenter, Humphrey and Mari Prichard, *The Oxford Companion to Children's Literature* (Oxford: Oxford University Press, 1984). A superb guide to the subject, covering authors, illustrators, characters, and texts. Informative entries covering the range of children's literature, from the earliest examples to the present day.

Carpenter, H., *Secret Gardens: A Study of the Golden Age of Children's Literature* (London: George Allen and Unwin, 1985). Carpenter provides highly enjoyable and insightful discussions of the writers who are associated with the 'Golden Age of children's literature' and their predecessors (from Kingsley to A. A. Milne). He's also interested in the pheno- menon of the 'Beautiful Child'. A must for anyone interested in children's literature.

Chambers, A., *Introducing Books to Children* (London: Heinemann Educational, 1973).

Chodorow, N., *The Reproduction of Mothering: Psychoanalysis and the Sociology of Gender* (Berkeley and Los Angeles: University of California Press, 1978).

Cott, Nancy F., 'Passionlessness: An Interpretation of Victorian Sexual Ideology, 1790–1850', in *Signs*, vol. 4, no. 2 (1978), pp. 219-36.

Coveney, P. *The Image of Childhood* (Harmondsworth: Penguin, 1967).

Cruse, A., *The Victorians and Their Books* (London: George Allen and Unwin, 1935).

Cutt, N. M., *Ministering Angels: A study of nineteenth-century evangelical writing for children* (Wormley, Hertfordshire: Five Owls Press, 1979).

Davidoff, Leonore, 'Class and Gender in Victorian England', in *Sex and Class in Women's History*, ed. J. Newton, M. Ryan and J. Walkwitz (London: Routledge and Kegan Paul, 1983).

Dickinson, P., 'A Defence of Rubbish', in *Writers, Critics and Children* (London: Heinemann Educational, 1976).

Dusinberre, Juliet, *Alice to the Lighthouse: Children's Books and Radical Experiments in Art* (London: Macmillan, 1987). Dusinberre is interested in the modernist period and so takes a sideways look at the influence on modernist writers of the books they read as children, and the relationship between adult and juvenile fiction of this period (for instance, the similarities between Frances Hodgson Burnett and D. H. Lawrence). Some fascinating ideas and material, though it helps if you know something about the writers of this period.

Dyhouse, C., *Girls Growing Up in Late Victorian and Edwardian England* (London: Routledge and Kegan Paul, 1981).

Eagleton, T., *Literary Theory: An Introduction* (Oxford: Basil Blackwell, 1983).

Ellis, A., *The History of Children's Reading and Literature* (London: Pergamon Press, 1969).

Fisher, M., *The Bright Face of Danger* (London: Hodder and Stoughton, 1986).

Foucault, M., trans. as *The Order of Things: An Archaeology of the Human Sciences* (1966; London: Tavistock, 1970).

Fox, G., *et al.* (eds), *Writers, Critics, and Children* (London: Heinemann Educational, 1976).

Frey, C., and J. Griffith, *The Literary Heritage of Childhood: An Appraisal of Children's Classics in the Western Tradition* (London: Greenwood Press, 1987).

Gifford, D., *Victorian Comics* (London: George Allen and Unwin, 1976).

Goldstrom, J. M., *Education: Elementary Education 1780–1900* (Newton Abbot: David and Charles, 1972).

Goodson, I., and Ball S. (eds), *Defining the Curriculum: Histories and Ethnographies* (Barcombe: Falmer Press, 1984).

Gorham, D., *The Victorian Girl and the Feminine Ideal* (London: Croom Helm, 1982).

Horn, Pamela, *The Victorian Country Child* (Gloucester: Alan Sutton, 1985). A good general introduction to nineteenth-century childhood which looks at education, living conditions, work, church, death and disease, and the legal position of the child. Very readable and includes some useful charts and documents.

Houghton, W. E., *The Victorian Frame of Mind, 1830-1870* (London: Yale University Press, 1957).

Howarth, P., *Play Up and Play the Game: The heroes of popular fiction* (London: Eyre Methuen, 1973).

Humphries, S., *Hooligans or Rebels? An oral history of working-class childhood and youth 1889-1939* (Oxford: Basil Blackwell, 1981).

Humphries, S., J. Mack, and R. Perks, *A Century of Childhood* (London: Sidgwick and Jackson, 1988). This book was written to accompany a Channel 4 series on the history of childhood. It is well illustrated and informative, covering nineteenth-century family life, school, games, and gangs.

Hunt, P. (ed.), *Children's Literature: The development of criticism* (London: Routledge, 1990).

Hunt, P., *Criticism, Theory, and Children's Literature* (Oxford: Basil Blackwell, 1991).

Hunt, P. (ed.) *Literature for Children: Contemporary Criticism* (London: Routledge, 1992).

Lacan, J., *Écrits*, trans. A. Sheridan (London: Tavistock, 1977).

Landsberg, Michele, *The World of Children's Books: A Guide to Choosing the Best* (London: Simon and Schuster, 1989). Some good essays on well-established sub-genres and more than 400 descriptions of 'good' children's books. Useful, but the booklist is rapidly dating. I prefer the annually revised *Children's Books of the Year*, selected by Julia Eccleshare (London: Anderson Press).

Leeson, R. (ed.), *Children's Books and Class Society Past and Present* (London: Children's Rights Workshop, 1977).

Lurie, Alison, *Don't Tell the Grown-Ups* (also published as *Not in Front of the Grown-Ups*) (London: Bloomsbury, 1990). An entertaining and eclectic collection of essays on some writers and aspects of children's literature. The general thesis is interesting: that most well-loved children's fiction challenges adult values.

McRobbie, A., and M. Nava, (eds), *Gender and Generation* (London: Macmillan, 1984).

Mayhew, H., *London Labour and the London Poor*, 4 vols (London, 1861-2; repr. New York: Dover Publications, 1968).

Meek, M., *On Being Literate* (London: Bodley Head, 1991).

Meek, M., A. Warlow, and G. Barton, *The Cool Web: The pattern of children's reading* (London: Bodley Head, 1977).

Meigs, C. (ed.), *A Critical History of Children's Literature: A survey of children's books in English from earliest times to the present* (London: Macmillan, 1953).

Michie, H., *The Flesh Made Word: Female Figures and Women's Bodies* (Oxford: Oxford University Press, 1987).

Mitterauer, M., *A History of Youth*, trans. G. Dunphy (1986; Oxford: Blackwell, 1992).

Muir, P., *English Children's Books 1600–1900* (London: Batsford, 1954).

Musgrave, P. W., *From Brown to Bunter: The life and death of the school story* (London: Routledge and Kegan Paul, 1985).

Opie, Iona and Peter, *The Lore and Language of Schoolchildren* (Oxford: Oxford University Press, 1959). The classic study of children's games and 'self-amusements'. The history of all kinds of play activities – from nursery rhymes and skipping games through nicknames, rituals, pranks, and torments – is explored. The Opies' most important findings were to do with the continuity and transmission of childhood activities.

Opie, I., *The People in the Playground* (Oxford: Oxford University Press, 1993). Iona Opie continues the work begun with her late husband by studying children at play at the end of the twentieth century. Her interest in this study was to set play activities in a living context. Fun to read and well observed.

Pinchbeck, I., and M. Hewitt, *Children in English Society*, 2 vols (London: Routledge and Kegan Paul, 1978).

Pollock, Linda, *Forgotten Children: Parent–Child Relationships from 1500–1900* (Cambridge: Cambridge University Press, 1983). Pollock disputes the arguments set out by Ariès in *Centuries of Childhood*, contending that there have always been childish children and loving parents.

Purvis, J., 'The Experience of Schooling for Working-Class Boys and Girls in Nineteenth-Century England', in *Defining the Curriculum: Histories and Ethnographies'*, ed. I. Goodson and S. Ball (Barcombe: Falmer Press, 1984).

Reynolds, Kimberley, *Girls Only? Gender and Popular Children's Fiction in Britain 1880-1910* (Hemel Hempstead: Harvester, 1990). Looks at the history of children's book publishing and some of the best-selling authors of the late-Victorian period. The suggestion is that attitudes to gender which evolved at this time continue to dominate writing for young people at the end of the twentieth century.

Reynolds, K., and N. Humble, *Victorian Heroines: Readings and Representations of Femininity in Nineteenth-Century Literature and Art* (Hemel Hempstead: Harvester, 1993).

Rose, J., *The Case of 'Peter Pan', or, The Impossibility of Children's Fiction* (London: Macmillan, 1984).

Rose, L., *The Erosion of Childhood: Child oppression in Britain 1860–1918* (London: Routledge, 1991).

Rosenthal, L., 'The Development of Consciousness in Lucy Boston's *The Children of Green Knowe*', in *The Modern Language Association's Children's Literature Association Journal* (Newhaven, Conn. and London: Yale University Press, 1980).

Rustin, Margaret, and Michael, *Narratives of Love and Loss: Studies in Modern Children's Fiction* (London: Verso, 1987). Psychoanalytic readings of a wide range of twentieth-century children's literature. Convincing and insightful.

Sarland, C., *Young People Reading: Culture and Response* (Milton Keynes: Open University Press, 1991).

Shavit, Z., *The Poetics of Children's Literature* (Athens, Ga: University of Georgia Press, 1986).

Showalter, E., *Sexual Anarchy: Gender and culture at the fin de siècle* (London: Virago, 1992).

Sinfield, A. (ed.), *Society and Literature 1945–1970* (London: Methuen, 1983).

Sommerville, C. J., *The Discovery of Childhood in Puritan England* (London: University of Georgia Press, 1992).

Stephens, J., *Language and Ideology in Children's Fiction* (London: Longman, 1992).

Stevenson, R., *Modernist Fiction: An Introduction* (Hemel Hempstead: Harvester, 1992).

Steedman, C., C. Urwin, and V. Walkerdine (eds), *Language, Gender and Childhood* (London: Routledge and Kegan Paul, 1984).

Stone, L., *The Family, Sex and Marriage in England 1500–1800* (London: Weidenfeld and Nicolson, 1977).

Tatar, M., *Off With Their Heads! Fairy tales and the culture of childhood* (London: Princeton University Press, 1992).

Taylor, G. Rattray, *The Angel Makers: A Study in the Psychological Origins of Historical Change, 1750-1850* (London: Secker and Warburg, 1973).

Thomas, K., 'Children in Early Modern England', in G. Avery and J. Briggs (eds), *Children and Their Books: A Celebration of the Work of Iona and Peter Opie* (Oxford: Clarendon Press, 1989). An excellent, concise and entertaining history of childhood from 1500 to 1800 (though he manages to bring in much more recent work as well). Looks at attitudes to childhood, education, children's letters and diaries, activities, and a wide range of documentary and anecdotal evidence about children in this period.

Townsend, John Rowe, *Written for Children: An outline of English-language Children's Literature* (London: Kestrel, 1965). This book has been revised several times since it first came out in 1965. It is a useful handbook which provides some interesting historical information about prominent authors and texts.

Tucker, N., *The Child and the Book: A psychological and literary exploration* (Cambridge: Cambridge University Press, 1981).

Tucker, N. (ed.), *Suitable for Children? Controversies in Children's Literature* (Brighton: Sussex University Press, 1976).

Walkerdine, V., 'On the Regulation of Speaking and Silence: Subjectivity, Class and Gender in Contemporary Schooling', in *Language, Gender and Childhood* ed. C. Steedman, C. Urwin, and V. Walkerdine (London, 1984).

Whitehead, F., A. C. Capey, W. Maddren, and A. Wellings (eds), *Children and Their Books: The final report of the Schools' Council research project on children's reading habits, 10-15* (London: Macmillan Educational, 1977).

Wilde, Oscar, *Complete Works of Oscar Wilde*, intro. Vyvyan Holland (London: Collins, 1969).

OTHER RELEVANT WORKS

Fin de siècle and modernism

Two books which will give a good general understanding of this period and its literary manifestations are:

Bradbury, M., and J. McFarlane, (eds) *Modernism: 1890–1930* (Harmondsworth: Pelican, 1976). A comprehensive study of the development of modernism in Europe. Discussion of the arts as well as literature. Needs to be read in small sections, and often assumes some general knowledge of the period.

Stevenson, Randall, *Modernist Fiction: An Introduction* (Hemel Hempstead: Harvester, 1992). A good general introduction to the ideas, influences, issues, and authors of the *fin de siècle* and early twentieth century.

Graphic novels and comics

Barker, Martin, *Comics: Ideology, Power and the Critics* (Manchester University Press, 1989). Particularly good on how readers read comics and the use of stereotypes.

Barker, Keith, *Graphic Account* (Newcastle-under-Lyme: Youth Libraries Group, 1993). A good introduction to the subject. Some straightforward essays and an excellent annotated bibliography.

Reynolds, Richard, *Superheroes* (London: Batsford, 1992). Helpful hints on how to read comics – particularly the outfits worn by the protagonists.

Specialist studies of picture books

Doonan, J., *Looking at Pictures in Picturebooks* (Stroud: Thimble Press, 1993).

Graham, J., *Pictures on the Page* (Sheffield: NATE, 1990).

Moebius, W., 'Introduction to Picture Book Codes', in *Word and Image*, vol. 2, no. 2, (1986), pp. 141-58.

Moss, G., 'Metafiction, Illustration, and the Poetics of Children's Literature', in P. Hunt (ed.), *Literature for Children: Contemporary Criticism* (London: Routledge, 1992).

Pinsent, P. (ed.), *The Power of the Page: Children's Books and Their Readers* (London: Fulton, 1993).

Whalley, J., and T. Chester, *A History of Children's Book Illustration* (London: Murray, 1988).

Index